TAKE IT TO THE MAT

by
Bobby Douglas
Head Coach, Iowa State University
Olympic Coach 1992

illustrated with
Les Anderson
NCAA Champion

edited by
Gretchen Topp

Published by
Sigler Printing & Publishing
Ames, Iowa

Also by the author:

Wrestling — The Making of a Champion: The Takedown

Wrestling — The Making of a Champion: Pinning and Olympic Freestyle Techniques

Wrestling — The Sunkist Kids Takedown System: Takedown II

Library of Congress Cataloging-in-Publication Data

Douglas, Bobby, 1942-
    Take it to the mat / Bobby Douglas ; illustrated with Les Anderson
; edited by Gretchen Topp. -- 1st ed.
        p.   cm.
    Includes index.
    ISBN 0-9635812-0-1
        1. Wrestling. 2. Wrestling--Rules.   I. Topp, Gretchen.
II. Title.
GV1195.D65   1993
796.8'12--dc20   92-84134
                                                                          CIP

Printed in the USA.

ACKNOWLEDGMENTS

This book is based on my technique, developed over a lifetime of wrestling competitively and coaching. I did not learn to wrestle by myself. I was fortunate enough to have excellent coaches, tutors and mat partners during my career.

I wish to thank the following people, to whom I owe a large part of my success: my family, Jackie and Bob ("Bo"); and Fred Davis, Anthony Davis, George Kovalick and Myron Roderick, who gave me a strong foundation in the sport.

Also, thanks to my students, who continue to help me learn.

APPRECIATIONS

I would like to thank Ron McMillen, publisher, Dave Popelka, Gretchen Topp, Coleen Nelson and the staff of Sigler Printing & Publishing for their work in producing this book.

I would also like to thank Art Martori and James Hathaway.

For additional technique illustrations, I would like to thank George Espinoza, Rick Iverson, Billy Rosado and Dan Severn.

PHOTO CREDITS

Howard Ferguson, *Edge*
Ernie Fulton
Ron Good, *Amateur Wrestling News*
Iowa State University Photo Service
Magnum, Inc.
Henry Marsh
Nadezhela Mischenko, Russia
Boyd Nelson
Cal Pokas, *Martins Ferry Times Leader*
George Tiedemann, *Sports Illustrated*
Randy Tomars
Bill Van Horne, *Wheeling News Register*
USA Wrestling

CONTENTS

PREFACE

Mat wrestling is becoming increasingly important as rule changes reward mat technique. The wrestler who is able to score on the mat is always dangerous.

The purpose of this book is to point out the key components of the techniques of mat wrestling. I have presented the holds in a step-by-step progression along with the drills and counters. It is important that you be able to change one hold into another so that you can develop continuous movement. (This is called *chain wrestling*.) Once you've learned to do this, you can scramble and move from one hold to the next, making it very difficult for your opponent.

Wrestling is, and will forever remain, a science, and we, the coaches and wrestlers, must adapt in order to compete in the twenty-first century.

The coach is the key to developing the plan. Success depends upon a good working relationship between the coach and student; this will have a lasting effect upon the wrestler's success. Strategy is the most difficult phase of wrestling to master. It requires a coach who is able to recognize the physical and emotional traits of a student's training timetable. He must weed out the weak points and substitute them with strong, sound concepts.

Wrestling provides a sense of values, a purpose, a belonging, a sense of being someone. If a wrestler is coachable, he can adapt to any situation. A wrestler must have mind control and proper focus. He has to know how to lose and come back. Wrestling develops loyalty to yourself and to all those dependent upon you. It produces self-respect.

Weakness—as well as strength—stems from the trait loosely known as disposition. No matter what the physical ability of a man, he cannot be a successful wrestler unless he has the disposition to be one. He must be of the frame of mind to want to wrestle, to run, to go through the long, grueling hours of practice, which is the only way to bring about perfection of detail. A successful hold is only attained by perfection of all detail.

It is only from a man's disposition that he gathers the strength to meet the stresses and crucial moments that come to all human beings. Commitment is one of the keys to becoming a champion. You must earn the right to be called a wrestler. This means that you pay the price of full practice, of strict training, and of belief in your teammates and in those people who guide your destiny.

(It is only from a man's disposition that he is empowered to go through each day's job and give it everything he possesses.)

You can master the fundamental techniques of wrestling only through drills and persistent rehearsal. Mastering mat techniques will make you a much better wrestler.

Bobby Douglas
Ames, Iowa
March 1993

DEDICATION

This book is dedicated to Coach George Kovalick and the American Cancer Society.

April 8, 1923
April 8, 1984

GEORGE KOVALICK AND THE BRIDGEPORT HIGH WRESTLING SQUAD

1959 Bridgeport High School Wrestling Squad

Bobby Douglas

There are many old-timers and Ohio Valley sports historians who firmly believe that the number one achievement ever attained by an Ohio Valley high school athletic team occurred at St. John's Arena in Columbus, Ohio, on a wintry February night in 1959. That night, a small band of wrestlers and their coach, George Kovalick, stunned state sports circles by coming out of a field of more than 100 schools to win the Ohio Wrestling Championships for Bridgeport High, a small school near Wheeling, West Virginia.

What made the Bridgeport Bulldogs' feat especially notable was the fact that at that time *all* schools, regardless of size, competed in the *same* state tournament field—not in three separate classes, as is the case today.

State wrestling meets had been held since 1938, but until Bridgeport had prevailed in 1959, the big schools from Cleveland had always dominated the tourney. Add to that the fact that Kovalick had introduced the sport to Bridgeport only nine years earlier, and one can see that the Bulldogs' victory was a genuine miracle.

Still, Bridgeport's success was no fluke. For years to come, the team was a wrestling presence in Ohio state tournaments, placing second in 1960 and third in 1961. And tiny Bridgeport was coming up a winner in other sports as well. It was even turning up star student athletes with real superstar potential—for example John Havlicek of the Boston Celtics and the Niekro brothers of major league baseball fame. In wrestling, I was fortunate enough to learn from George Kovalick. He introduced me to wrestling technique, polished my skills and set me on a journey that would lead to five national titles, Olympic team captain in 1968, and outstanding wrestler in 1970.

One has to ask how one small town suddenly wound up with all this talent. Bridgeport had become one of those rare and curious local hotspots that mysteriously becomes a kind of focal point for sports magic. It's not really going to far to say that the sports achievements of this town during the fifties bordered on the supernatural.

This is not to say, however, that we can't find an explanation if we look closely. Clearly, the answer has something to do with George Kovalick, the head coach and architect for many of Bridgeport's winning teams. Quite simply, Kovalick brought out the best in the young athletes he coached. He was more than a coach: he was a teacher who taught his students about purpose in life. He taught them how to find a goal and center themselves around it. He inspired them to reach for their full potential. In other words, Kovalick had the special vision that it takes to see, touch and guide the spirit in men. It was *his* magic, perhaps more than anything else, that made Bridgeport great.

State tournament: Saint John's Arena, Ohio State University

A LETTER TO COACH KOVALICK

Dear Coach,

I understand that you were honored at a dinner the other night. I just wanted to add my congratulations.

I think you can count the people who have a major influence in your life on one hand and sometimes have fingers left over. I wasn't able to appreciate it at the time, but you were one of those people for me. In retrospect, it was the first time we were treated as adults. Two things I recall quite vividly that happened over 23 years ago. The first was a lesson about being a winner versus quitting. I believe it was half-time during a game at Tiltonsville. It was a statement you made about losing control, about not concentrating on the task at hand, about losing sight of our purpose. (Not eloquently stated.)

The second time was on a bus during my junior year. We were on our way to a match at Steubenville. Fred Fox was late to meet the bus. I was truly afraid I would have to wrestle in his place. You were upset with me, and I was embarrassed and angry with myself. Seems very simple and certainly not memorable. But it stuck with me. Every time I'm frightened or anxious about some task, I still think about that time and my feelings. It drives me on because I was frightened then and overcame it and I can do it again and again.

You have every reason to be proud of what you've accomplished, not only with your teams but the kids you helped to be men. There are a lot of us who are much better folks for your contact and assistance.

I understand you are having a match of your own with cancer. I experienced a similar one 15 years ago. Very difficult to go through those treatments, but somehow you come through them. I would only hope that my encouragement would have half the impact that yours did on me.

By the way, Fox didn't show up. I had to wrestle, and I lost big. But I got through it. I didn't think I could, but I did.

I hope you are able to find that kind of courage in your fight.

May God bless you and yours and be with you through your ordeal.

Ron Scott
Class of 1962
Bridgeport High

COACH KOVALICK'S RESPONSE — April 3, 1984

Dear Ron,

Sorry I'm late in answering your letter. I was in the hospital receiving a chemo treatment. I was quite surprised, but it was a pleasant surprise and I want to thank you for all those nice remarks. Someone once told me that a teacher or coach never really knows what influence he has on a person until 20 or 30 years later. I must say that I've been overwhelmed by all the positive statements from former students and athletes like yourself. It makes me feel that life has been worth living and that, together, we've all accomplished something that has made our lives richer.

Your comments about the football game and wrestling match were most interesting. It's difficult for me to remember that far back, but after reading your letter I could recall the incidents quite clearly. I'm glad that they had a positive effect on you. And while we're on the subject of wrestling, Ron, I've learned a few things over the years. It's easy for a winner to walk out on the mat. It's tough to walk out there when you know that you can't win. That takes courage.

I was also quite surprised that you had a bout with cancer several years ago. I'm so happy that you made it. You are a nice person and much too young to die. Your athletic training and background may have helped you. We can relate to each other on this subject. Cancer is what I call the bastard disease—the disease is hell and the treatment is hell. Mine started with a tumor in the eye and then it spread to the liver, which is always fatal. (In spite of all the treatments I've had, my body tells me that I don't have much more time.) This is like walking out on the mat knowing that you can't win. I believe that the discipline I learned in athletics, a great family and friends like yourself have helped to sustain me throughout this trying ordeal. And I hope that when my time comes, I can face up to it with dignity and courage.

Thanks again, Ron, for your very nice letter and comments and I want to wish you and your family the very best of luck and an interesting and exciting future.

Sincerely,
The Old Coach
George Kovalick

GEORGE KOVALICK

I was very fortunate to have a coach whose philosophy and methods provided me with the wisdom that has been most responsible for my success. The following are some excerpts from his notes; these were my coach's words. They have served me well in the past and now guide me in the present.

Thanks, Coach.

COACH SAID:

ATHLETE:

Go to practice. Work hard. Always give it your best shot.

COACH:

Organize the program. You have to know what to teach. Teach the fundamentals.

DAD:

Teach him discipline and respect. Make him go to practice.

MOM:

Keep everything in proper perspective.

ATHLETES:

Have fun (training, discipline, strength).

I LOOK FOR AN ATHLETE WHO:

1. Is consistent at practice.
2. Works hard and tries his best, who has a good attitude, is positive.
3. Recognizes that he will have to work and sacrifice to be a champion (five to seven years).
4. Gives himself a fair chance. Don't quit too soon.

RULES OF CONDUCT (ACCUSED OF BEING TOUGH)

1. No smoking, drinking or drugs.
2. Associate with good people.
3. Be home by 9 p.m.
4. Maintain a "B" average.
5. Never miss practice.

KNOW WHAT TO EXPECT WHEN YOU GET TO HIGH SCHOOL

1. Be able to cope.
2. Success in grade school does not mean success in high school. The same is true for college.
3. Competition gets tougher, for example, wrestling at the national tournament.

LONG TOUGH ROAD TO ANY CHAMPIONSHIP

1. It can't be done overnight.
2. There are no shortcuts.
3. There is no instant success.

ADVICE FOR PARENTS

1. Be interested.
2. Attend and support.
3. Don't criticize for physical mistakes.
4. Don't apply undue pressure—pressure can ruin an athlete.
5. Mom can help (as a good stabilizing force).

It is a tragedy that over 50% of junior high athletes drop out. I have never coached an athlete who couldn't make a team. It didn't make any difference how big, or small or slow he was. [Coach said, "It isn't the size of the dog in the fight but the fight in the dog."] There is only one reason for quitting: You don't like the sport.

COACH KOVALICK'S LAST WORDS

The time has come, and I need to say some things:

Bill Van Horne, thank you for the support you have given me and for the way you have supported athletics in the Valley.

The greatest reward for me has been the number of former students and athletes who have become successful and outstanding in their respective fields. The future belongs to them, and I feel confident that they will be able to handle it.

I apologize if I mistreated or offended anyone. I tried to make my athletes better people, teach them to work hard. I tried to get them to reach their potential. I tried to give everyone an opportunity.

Prayers—the Ten Commandments are great advice to follow.

What is our purpose in life? I have been to the mountain top of athletics.

I apologize for my mistakes. I did what I thought was right, what I would have done myself. You never know whether you did justice or not until 25 or 30 years later. Never miss practice.

People come and go. In the final analysis, ideas, achievements and accomplishments remain. It's not what I did for athletics, it's what athletics has done for my family and me.

From the day I entered college in the fall of 1946 to prepare for my life's work, I knew that I wanted to teach and coach. I have never deviated from that objective. I feel fortunate in that I was able to do what I wanted to do. Many people never get that opportunity. It has made for a very rich and rewarding life. My sincere gratitude to the athletes and sports fans.

Bobby Douglas & Dan Gable at the
1968 Olympic trials

1968 Olympic trials

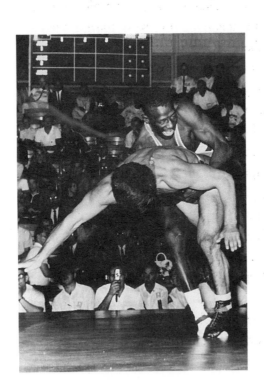

HOW TO USE THIS BOOK

Many of the photographs in this book feature horizontal and vertical lines in the background. These lines will guide you in determining the distance covered in a given move. The blocks of the grid measure one meter. The horizontal lines on the wall represent upward and downward motion.

From the other lines, you can gauge the forward and circular motion. The numbered sections on the grid assist in calculating the distance moved. For example, you can judge the distance covered by the wrestler as well as his accompanying vertical movements.

1

2

3

Les Anderson demonstrating a foot-block breakdown (figures 1-3). *Note the movement of the body across the grid.*

Kenny Monday and Nate Carr

MAT WRESTLING
TECHNIQUES

Bobby Douglas and Bill Smith

THE TOP MAN
STARTING POSITION*

OFFENSIVE WRESTLER.

(1) The offensive wrestler shall be on the right or left side of his opponent with at least one knee on the mat and his head above the mid line of his opponent's back. One arm (right or left) is placed loosely around the defensive wrestler's body perpendicular to the long axis of the body, with the palm of the hand placed loosely against the defensive wrestler's navel and the palm of his other hand (left or right) placed on or over the back of the near elbow, this being the near side. One knee shall be on the mat to the outside of the near leg, not touching the defensive wrestler; and a knee or foot may be placed in back of the defensive wrestler's feet, not touching the defensive wrestler

(2) *Optional offensive starting position.* The offensive wrestler may use an optional start whereby he positions himself on either side or to the rear of his opponent supporting all his weight on both feet, one knee or both knees. He is to place his hands on his opponent's back (area between neck and waist), thumbs touching, and only his hands are to be in contact with the defensive wrestler. The offensive wrestler is not to place his foot or feet, or knee(s), between his opponent's feet or legs, nor may he straddle his opponent.

(3) The referee is authorized to direct the offensive man to take a starting position after the defensive man is stationary in his starting position on the mat.

*Disclaimer: This material subject to annual review and change. Permission to reprint granted by NCAA.

"The man who says it cannot be done should not interrupt the man doing it."
— *Chinese proverb*

TIPS FOR THE TOP MAN POSITION

Remove whatever is supporting your opponent. Consider the man underneath as a four-legged table in learning breakdowns.

If you can maintain a tight position on him, he will burn up more energy as he carries you and attempts to score. Stay off both knees—make him carry your weight.

Move him on the whistle by driving your hips into him and pulling his elbow into his side (tuck position). Your initial drive should place your opponent's weight on his hands and knees.

If, on your initial attack, his base is so strong that you cannot break him down, move to the side and jerk his hips back into your lap. Once his hips touch the mat, you have to quickly cover them and try to tie up his hands, so that he cannot regain his base. One key to top control is to stay off your knees and constantly push off your toes, driving your chest into your opponent's back and hips. If he is using his hands to regain his base, you have the option of the near-wrist attack, crossface, or hand control. If you can maintain pressure with your chest and keep his head down, he will not be able to score.

Control your man at the waist or lower. Don't let him get his arms and legs free.

The man underneath will often relax momentarily out of bewilderment. This is a good time to continue your advantage by tying him up in a pin hold.

Rarely is it safe to apply a pinning hold on an opponent while he is on his knees. Break him down first.

Always anticipate the referee's whistle when you are in the starting position on the mat. Watch his lips, and, at the moment of his signal, move your man off balance.

Hook your man with your legs whenever possible. Relax when you are in control; you can follow his movements better that way.

When he is attempting side rolls, move to the side toward which he is rolling.

Keep him off balance, and work to cover his body. Force him to his belly and keep him there while you work for the pin. In pinning, control both the head and the crotch. Move perpendicularly and drive with your legs.

Put the half nelson in near your opponent's elbow and the top of his head.

Learn to change combinations faster than he can counter.

1

2

3

Don't stop before you hear the referee's whistle. Don't use up energy by tightening up. Don't complain to the official. Don't stop the clock by going off the mat when you are ahead and time is running out. It is wrong to ease up because your opponent has.

After going off the mat, jump to your feet and be the first one back to the center. This tactic helps you to keep your confidence as well as to discourage your opponent.

Always be ready to shift your base (and adjust your position to maintain your balance). Stay on your toes and drive with your chest and hips on top.

FALLS AND NEAR FALLS*

FALL

Any part of both shoulders or part of both scapulae held in contact with the mat for one second constitutes a fall. The one-second count (one-thousand-and-one) shall be a silent count by the referee and shall start only after the referee is in such position that he can observe that a fall is imminent, after which the shoulders or scapula area must be held in continuous contact with the mat in bounds for one second before a fall is awarded.

a. A fall shall not be awarded unless any part of both shoulders or part of both scapulae of the defensive wrestler are in bounds.

b. If either wrestler is handicapped by having any portion of his body out of bounds, no fall shall be awarded and out of bounds shall be declared.

c. When the match is stopped for out of bounds in a fall situation, the match shall be resumed in the starting position on the mat.

d. A fall will be indicated by the referee striking the mat with the palm of the hand.

e. When the referee is able to determine that a fall has occurred and the period ends before he can so indicate, the fall shall be awarded.

f. If the referee cannot determine that a fall has occurred before the period ends due to crowd noise or other circumstances, he shall consult with the assistant referee, if available. If there is no assistant or if the assistant referee is in doubt, the referee shall ask the match timekeeper whether the indication was made by hand signal before the period ended.

NEAR FALL

a. A near fall is a position in which the offensive wrestler has his opponent in a controlled pinning situation for two seconds and (1) the wrestler is held in a high bridge or on both elbows, or (2) one shoulder or the head is touching the mat and the other shoulder is held at an angle of 45 degrees or less to the mat, or (3) both shoulders or both scapulae are held

*Disclaimer: This material subject to annual review and change. Permission to reprint granted by NCAA.

within four inches of the mat. Two points shall be awarded for such near-fall situations. A continuous roll through is not to be considered a near fall.

b. The criteria for a near fall having been met uninterrupted for five seconds, three points shall be awarded. A verbal and, whenever possible, a visual hand count is to be used in determining a three-point near fall.

c. A near fall is ended when the defensive wrestler gets out of a pinning situation. The referee must not signal the score for a near fall until the situation is ended. Only one near fall shall be scored in each pinning situation, regardless of the number of times the offensive wrestler places the defensive wrestler in a near-fall position during the pinning situation.

Only the wrestler with the advantage, who has his opponent in a pinning situation, may score a near fall. Bridgebacks in body scissors or bridgeovers with a wristlock are not considered near-fall situations, even though a fall may be scored.

When the defensive wrestler places himself in a precarious situation during an attempted escape or reversal, particularly leg vines and body scissors, a near fall shall not be scored unless the offensive wrestler has control of and has definitely restrained his opponent in a pinning situation for two seconds.

d. When a pinning combination is legally executed by the contestant is injured before near-fall criteria are met and a near fall is imminent, action will be stopped and a two-point near fall shall be awarded.

e. Any time a hold is legally executed, criteria for a near fall are met for two seconds and a contestant is injured, action will stop and a three-point near fall shall be awarded.

Todd Kinney (top position)

PINNING TIPS FOR THE TOP POSITION

Pinning is the ultimate objective in wrestling, and all holds should lead to the pin.

Break your opponent down on his stomach and keep him there while you work for the pin. Move to a perpendicular position and drive with your legs. Control both the head and the hips. Place him in a second pin hold if he gets out of the first one. Stay away from his head when working from behind, unless absolutely necessary for a pin hold.

If he is using his elbows for support, get the wrist and drive. Use your chest to hold him on the mat. One important thing to remember is to change from side to side, so that he can never regain a good starting position. This must be your strategy. Stay off both knees, make him carry your weight. Constantly push off your toes, driving your chest and hips into him. If he is using his hands to regain his starting position, you have the options of the near-wrist, cross-face, or hand control. Maintain top pressure with your body and keep his head down. An example of this is to use your chest like a bulldozer, moving him forward, driving with your toes and forcing his body into the mat with your body.

Matt Johnson (top position)

If your shoulder touches the mat for one second, you're pinned in college; high school, two seconds; international, less than a second.

NEAR-WRIST

From the top position *(figures 1-3)*, reach inside your opponent's crotch and under the knee. Spin him to the mat *(figures 4-6; continued on following pages).*

1

2

3

4

5

6

NEAR-WRIST

CONTINUED

Catch his wrist and drive his shoulder to the mat *(figures 7-12; continued on next page)*.

7

8

The near-wrist attack: If your opponent is using his elbows for support from a belly-down position, use your chest to hold him on the mat. Attack with the cross-face or the half nelson.

9

10

11

12

NEAR-WRIST

CONTINUED

Reach inside his crotch and under his knee.
Lift his legs; release his arm for back points
(figures 13-20).

13

14

15

16

17

18

19

20

CRADLE

The bottom man moves to his hands and feet. Overhook his head; lock your hands at the knee. Drive your forehead into his hip *(figures 1-5; continued on next page).*

1

2

3

4

5

CRADLE
CONTINUED

Sit under his leg, look up, drive backwards and hook his free leg for the pin *(figures 6-12)*.

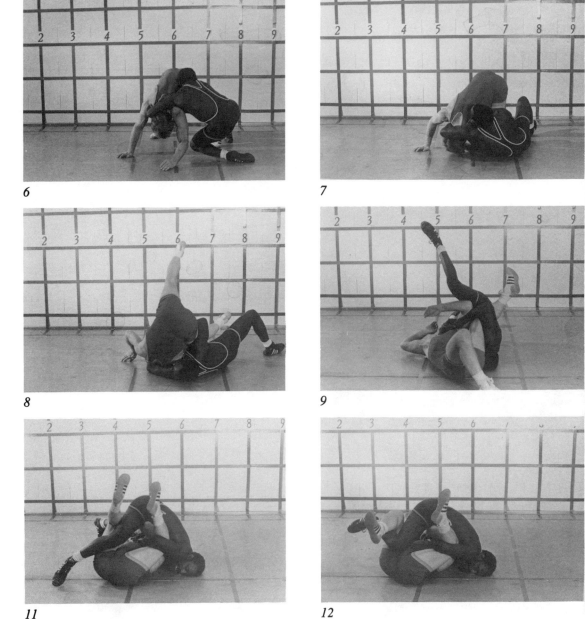

6

7

8

9

10

11

12

THREE-QUARTER NELSON

The bottom man moves to his hands and feet. Hook his near ankle with your leg (figures 1-6). Reach under his body and around his neck, and lock your hands (continued on next page).

Matt Johnson

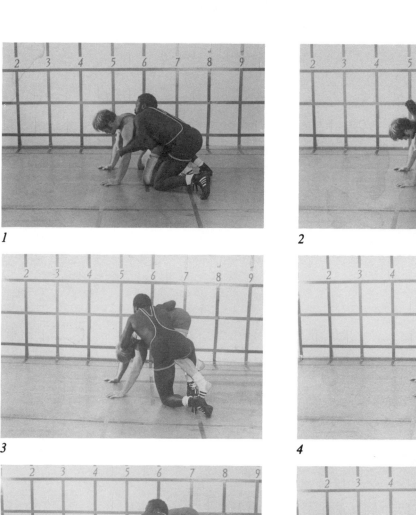

1

2

3

4

5

6

THREE-QUARTER NELSON

CONTINUED

Pull his head down by driving your shoulder into his side. Pull the leg toward his head until he is pinned (*figures 7-11*).

7

8

9

10

11

FAR SHOULDER AND ANKLE

From the top position, sit into your opponent. Catch his far ankle and shoulder, forcing his hands into the mat *(figures 1 and 2)*. Pull him into your lap, and hook the leg *(figures 3-6)*.

Drive your knee into your opponent's leg (figure 4).

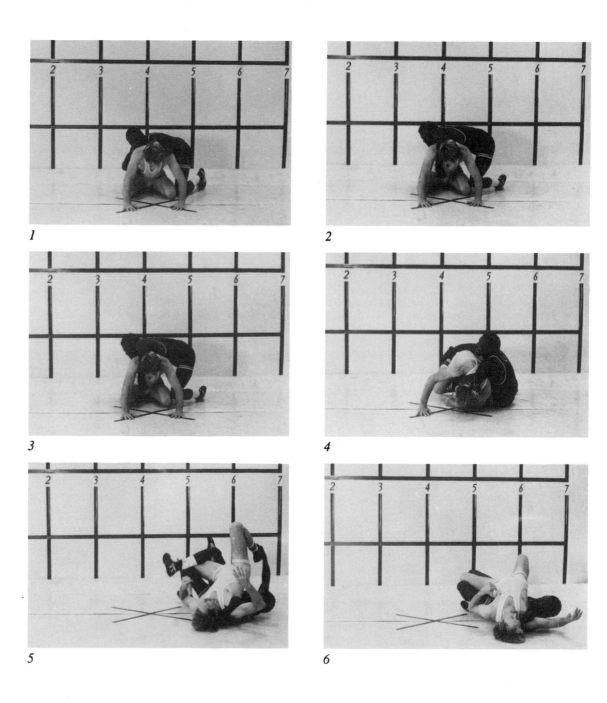

1

2

3

4

5

6

NEAR-ANKLE LIFT

From the top position, catch your opponent's ankle, reach inside his crotch, stand and lift the leg *(figures 1 and 2)*. Your right arm reaches inside the crotch, your left arm catches the far shoulder *(figure 3)*. Lift and step across the far leg *(figures 4 and 5)*. Lunge forward, throwing him to his back *(figures 6 and 7)*.

1

2

3

4

5

6

7

BREAKDOWNS

Kenny Monday (Top Position) Eddie Urbano

LEG SCISSOR ANKLE

From the top position, hook your opponent's leg with your leg. Catch his shoulder and lift his ankle *(figures 1 and 2)*. Force your hips into him. Arching your back, lift the leg to break him down *(figures 3 and 4)*.

The leg that is hooking your opponent must be high on the thigh. Your hips must be on top of your opponent's hips.

1

2

3

4

POWER HALF AND ANKLE HOOK

From the leg scissor, place your elbow behind your opponent's neck; lock your hands under his elbow. With your free leg, hook the ankle and lift. Arch your back and lift the inside leg to break him down.

Chain wrestling is essential to success in wrestling. Learn all holds in meaningful relation to other holds, not as isolated maneuvers. A hold should lead to a fall.

1

2

3

4

DOUBLE LEG SCISSOR

Using the leg scissor and ankle control, release the ankle, lock your hands under the elbow. Hook your free leg inside the crotch, and arch forward for the breakdown.

1

2

3

4

LEG SCISSOR WRIST

From the leg scissor, capture your opponent's wrist *(figures 1 and 2)*. Lunge forward and arch your back. Lift the leg to break his balance *(figures 3 - 5)*.

The hands are behind the arm (figures 2 and 3).

1

2

3

4

5

POWER HALF

From the leg scissor position, your arm is placed behind your opponent's neck and under his arm *(figure 1)*. Force your opponent's head down, lean over his head and lift his shoulder *(figures 2 and 3)*.

1

2

3

Bill Cripps (top position)

CROSSFACE

Using the leg scissor, arch your back and lunge across your opponent's body *(figures 1 and 2)*. Catch his head and pull him across *(figures 3 and 4)*. Release his head and hook his arm for the pin *(figure 5)*.

1

2

3

4

5

Adam Derengowski (top position)

CRADLE

From the leg scissor position, your opponent attempts to stand with his outside leg *(figure 1)*. Lock your hands around his neck and knee *(figures 2 and 3)*. Pull him into your lap, release the scissor and step across his free leg for the pin *(figures 4-6)*.

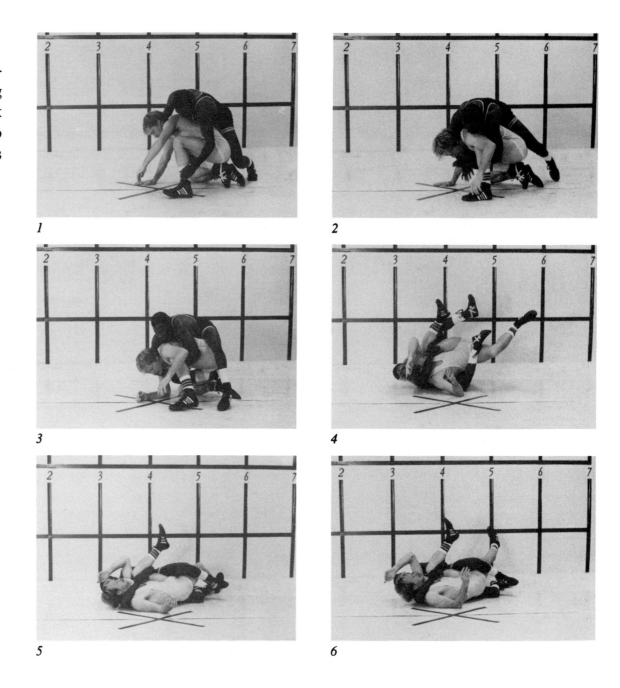

1

2

3

4

5

6

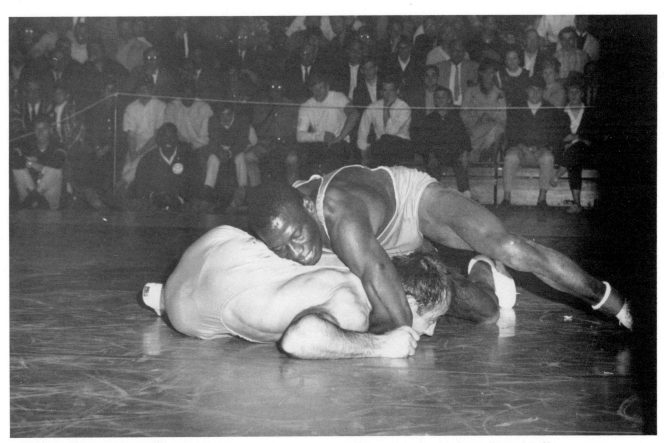

1968 AAU Wrestling Championship at Ames, Iowa - Bobby Douglas defeats Tom Huff.

THE BOTTOM MAN

STARTING POSITION*

DEFENSIVE WRESTLER.

The defensive wrestler takes a stationary position at the center of the mat in which he is on his hands and knees as directed by the referee. He must keep both knees on the mat even with and behind the rear starting line. The heels of both hands must be on the mat in front of the forward starting line. The elbows shall not touch the mat. This position also must allow the offensive wrestler to be able to assume a legal starting position on the side of his choice.

Start on your knees with your weight back, your head up and with little weight on your hands.

*Disclaimer: This material subject to annual review and change. Permission to reprint granted by NCAA.

ESCAPES AND REVERSALS*

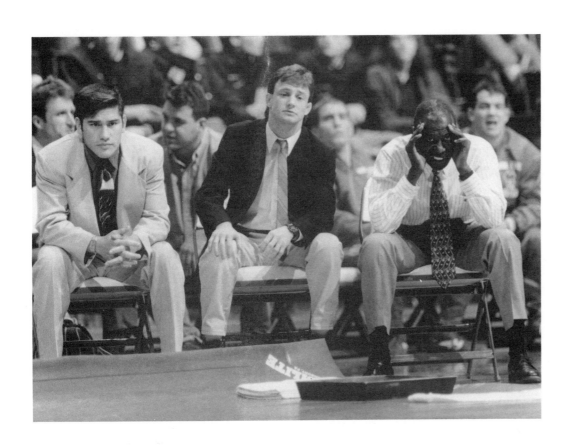

ESCAPE

An escape occurs when the defensive wrestler gains a neutral position and the offensive wrestler has lost control while the supporting points of either wrestler are in bounds.

REVERSAL

A reversal occurs when the defensive wrestler comes from underneath and gains control of his opponent, either on the mat or in a rear standing position.

For the purpose of awarding reversal points at the edge of the mat, such points shall be awarded when control is established while the supporting points of either wrestler are in bounds or while at least the feet of the scoring contestant remain down on the mat in bounds.

*Disclaimer: This material subject to annual review and change. Permission to reprint granted by NCAA.

BOTTOM MAN POSITION

Push back to stop your opponent's driving motion *(figure 4)*. Keep your toes tucked. Shift your weight onto your feet by arching your back and raising your head *(figures 5 and 6)*.

1

2

3

4

5

6

INSIDE LEG
STAND-UP SEQUENCE DRILL

Step up with your inside leg and control your opponent's hands.

This drill is to be repeated until perfected. The more repetitions, the better the chance of perfecting this technique.

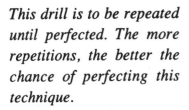

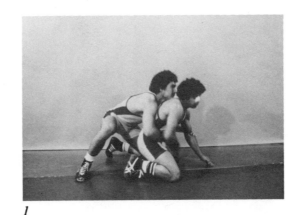

1

2

3

4

5

6

INSIDE LEG
FRONT VIEW

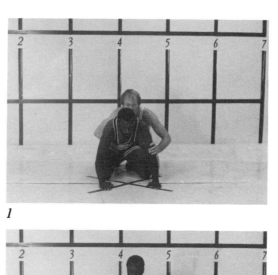

1

2

When you get to the standing position, keep your feet moving.

3

4

INSIDE LEG
OPPOSITE SIDE VIEW

Your opponent has control of your ankle *(figures 1-4)*. Catch his wrist and step up with your foot. Push back into a squat position and move your feet away. Step your legs under the knee to a face-off position *(figures 5 and 6)*.

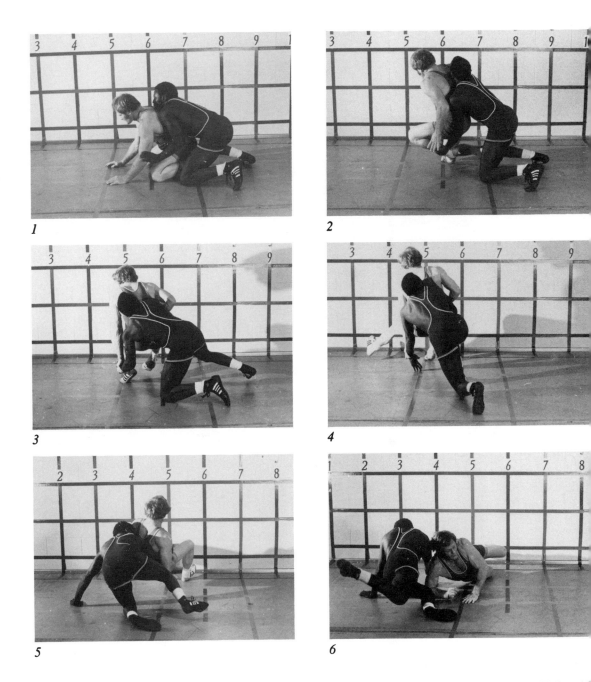

1

2

3

4

5

6

Gary Bohay (top position) and Barry Davis

OUTSIDE LEG

From the bottom position, move back, shift your weight into your opponent and raise your back *(figures 1-3)*. Your right foot replaces your left hand. *(Continued on next page.)*

1

2

3

Don't let your opponent drive you out of bounds.

OUTSIDE LEG

CONTINUED

Control his hands and stand *(figures 4-8).*

4

5

Note the distance of the hips and the back pressure (figure 7).

6

7

8

BREAKING ANKLE CONTROL

The top man controls your ankle. Position your hips on his arm *(figures 1-3)*. Push back into him; catch his wrist; back into a squat position and push up to your feet *(figures 4-6)*.

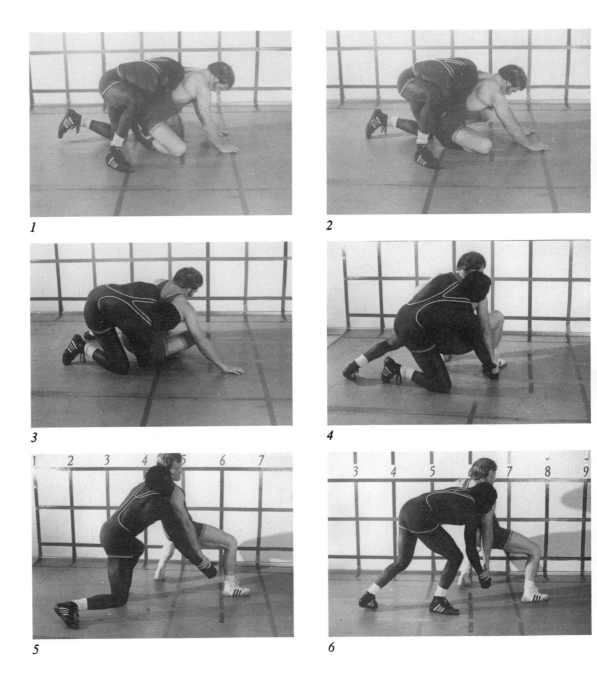

1

2

3

4

5

6

BREAKING ANKLE CONTROL

OPPOSITE SIDE VIEW

From the bottom position, move to a sit position, controlling his wrist *(figures 1-5; continued on next page).*

1

2

3

4

5

BREAKING ANKLE CONTROL

OPPOSITE SIDE VIEW, CONTINUED

Push back up to your feet *(figures 6-9)*.

6

7

8

9

PIVOT-OUT

Move your feet away, push back and control your opponent's wrist *(figures 1-5; continued on next page).*

Be able to stand by backing into your man with your feet in a wide position. If he forces into you, put one foot forward. If he breaks you down, turn and switch or roll. Try to stand again. Always fight his hands and push backwards to make him fight to hold on while you figure out your next attack.

1

2

3

4

5

PIVOT-OUT
CONTINUED

Move to a squat position, push back and stand *(figures 6-8)*.

6

7

8

It's important to hold the wrist for balance. Don't let your opponent lock his hands.

BREAKING A WAIST LOCK

From the standing defensive position (*figures 1-3*), move your feet to prevent your opponent from pushing you off the mat, tripping, or lifting you. Keep a wide stance with one foot forward (*figures 4 and 5*). Push back, squat and twist his hands apart; move your feet forward to break his grip (*figure 6; continued on next page*).

1

2

3

4

5

6

BREAKING A WAIST LOCK
CONTINUED

Reverse direction by stepping back to a face-off position *(figures 7-12)*.

Eric Akin

7

8

9

10

11

12

BREAKING A WAIST LOCK
FRONT VIEW

1

2

Back step (figures 2 and 3). *Don't let your opponent lock his hands.*

3

4

BREAKING A WAIST LOCK

REAR VIEW

1

2

3

SLIP THROUGH

From the standing position *(figures 1-3)*, your opponent's hands are locked around your chest. Squat, raise your arms over your head, lean back and pull them free. Sit-out and face-off for the escape *(figures 4 and 5)*.

Note figures 2 and 3. Squeeze down on the arms. Push back and squat.

1

2

3

4

5

STANDING SIDE ROLL

From the standing position *(figures 1-3)*, grab your opponent's wrist, pull it tight to your chest, squat and position your hips to the side. Catch his leg, kneel to your elbow and pull him over your back for the reversal *(figures 4-6)*.

Note the changed foot position in figures 3 and 4. When you kneel, position your head outside your opponent's knee and lift him over your back.

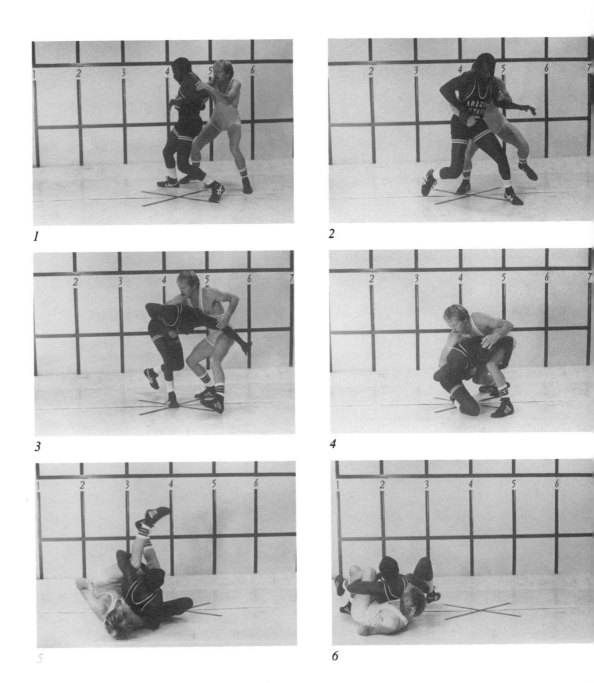

1

2

3

4

5

6

STANDING SIDE ROLL

From the standing position *(figures 1-3)*, control your opponent's wrist, blocking his thigh with your hand; push his leg away and turn. Place your instep on his thigh *(figures 4 and 5)*. Drop to your elbow, lift your foot, pull him over your back and move to a sit-out position.

Figure 1 is a good defense when your opponent is trying to break you down.

Note the footwork in figures 2 and 3.

1

2

3

4

5

STANDING ROLL

From the defensive position *(figures 1-3)*, control your opponent's wrist, squat and step behind his foot *(figures 4-6; continued on next page)*.

Note the position of Les's hips. The hip changes to the inside as he turns to drop.

1

2

3

4

5

6

STANDING ROLL
CONTINUED

Lean forward, drop to your elbow. Pull your opponent over your back and sit into him for the reversal *(figures 7-10).*

7

8

9

10

STAND-UP COUNTERS

Kenny Monday and Nate Carr

OUTSIDE TRIP

From the offensive position *(figures 1 and 2)*, pull your opponent's hips in, step around his leg, trip and drive forward *(figures 3-5)*.

1

2

3

4

5

SIT-THROUGH FOOT BLOCK

From the offensive position *(figures 1-4)*, your opponent attempts to break your grip. Step between his legs and drop under his hips *(continued on next page)*.

1

2

3

4

SIT-THROUGH FOOT BLOCK
CONTINUED

[r]am your right foot against the back of your
[o]pponent's ankle. Pull him over your body
[t]o break his balance. Place your free hand on
[t]he mat; swing your left knee between his
[l]egs to regain the top position *(figures 5-7)*.

6

7

SIDE LIFT

From the standing offensive position, your opponent attempts to break your grip. Step around his leg, thrust your hips in and lift.

1

2

3

4

5

6

7

8

SIDE LIFT
USING THE KNEE

From the standing offensive position *(figures 1 and 2)*, your opponent attempts to break your grip. Step around his leg, squat, and thrust your hips and leg in to lift *(figures 3-5)*.

1

2

3

4

5

SIT-OUT DRILL

From the bottom position, move your feet away and push back *(figures 1 and 2)*. Sit your left leg through, turn on your side and shoulder to a face-off position *(figures 3-5)*.

1

2

This drill is excellent for conditioning.

3

4

5

TURN-IN

From the bottom position *(figures 1 and 2)*, push back into your opponent, move your feet away and sit to your side *(figures 3 and 4)*. Drop your shoulder to the mat and turn to a face-off position for the escape *(figure 5)*.

This is a good technique when the top man goes after your ankle.

1

2

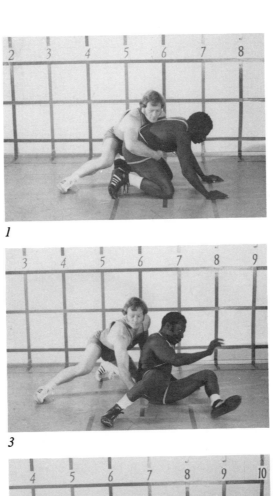

3

4

5

1

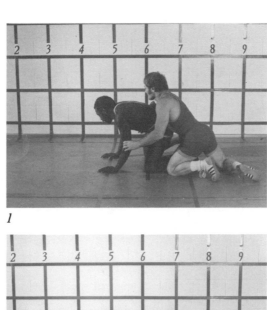

2

Note figure 3. Place your shoulder down on the mat. Throw your arm and knee toward your head on the turn.

3

4

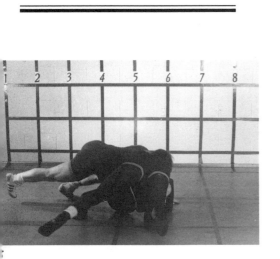

6

7

HEAD SPIN

From the bottom position *(figures 1-2)*, move your feet away and push back into your opponent. Sit to your side and turn on your shoulder *(figures 3-5)*. Move to your head and walk your feet away for the escape *(figures 6-7)*.

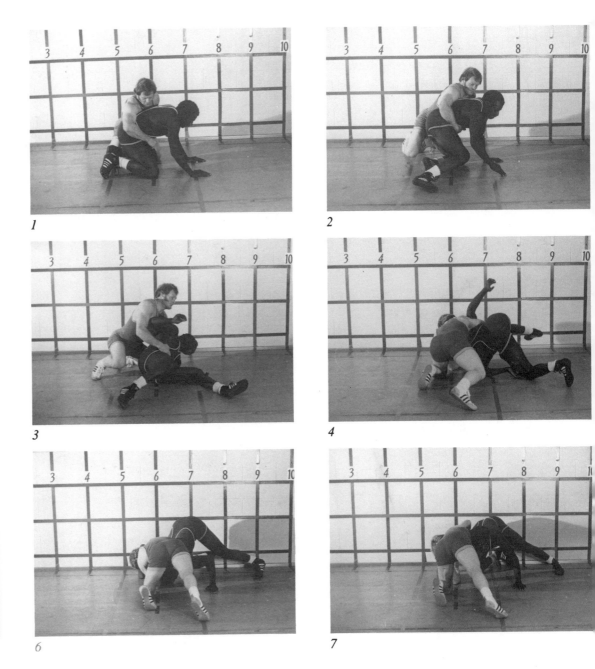

1

2

3

4

5

6

7

TURN-IN

From the sit position *(figures 1-3)*, turn on your elbow and step your leg under your knee. Raise your elbow and look up to get position for the reversal *(figures 4-7)*.

Note figure 5. This is where the top man is most likely to try a step-over counter. (See pages 121-23 for step-over counters.)

1

2

3

4

6

7

TURN-IN

OPPOSITE SIDE VIEW

From the bottom position, move to the sit-out position. Turn on your elbow and step your leg under your knee *(figures 1-6; continued on next page)*.

1

2

3

4

5

6

TURN-IN
OPPOSITE SIDE VIEW, CONTINUED

Raise your elbow and look up to get position for the reversal *(figures 7-9)*.

7

8

9

SIT-POSITION DRILL
FRONT VIEW

With this drill, you practice moving from a bottom position to a sit position.

1. *Keep your head up.*
2. *Keep your hips under you.*
3. *Be ready to turn or stand at all times.*

1

2

3

4

SHOULDER ROLL

From the sit position *(figures 1 and 2)*, roll across your shoulders, catch your opponent's leg *(figures 3-6)* and return to the sit position for the reversal *(figures 7 and 8)*.

You can get back points from this position.

1

2

4

5

7

8

SHOULDER ROLL

From the sit position, your opponent underhooks your arms and attempts to pull you back (figures 1-4). Catch his wrist, place your free hand on the mat, raise your hips and roll across your shoulders for the escape (figures 5 and 6).

It's important to hold the arm up to your chest.

Figure 4 shows the chin position.

Figure 6 shows the wrist control and arm position.

1

2

3

4

5

6

SHOULDER ROLL

From the sit position, catch your opponent's wrist and pull up *(figures 1-3)*. Tuck your chin to your chest, raise your hips and roll across your shoulders *(figures 4-6; continued on next page)*.

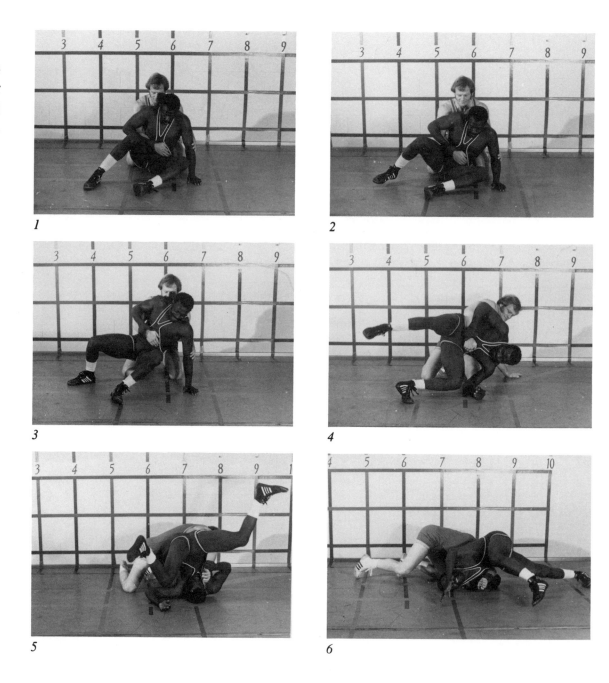

1

2

3

4

5

6

SHOULDER ROLL
CONTINUED

Catch his leg and move behind him *(figures 7-10)*.

These are the key points to remember when using this technique:

1. *Keep your chin tucked to your chest.*
2. *Roll across your neck and shoulders.*
3. *Use your legs like a cartwheel to get momentum.*
4. *Control the arm that's around your waist.*
5. *The best time to attempt this technique is when your opponent is trying to break you down.*

7

8

9

10

HIP HEIST DRILL

This drill is used to develop the sit-out and
roll techniques.

Always maintain a good bottom position. Return to your base after every sit-out.

2

3

Note how the foot steps under the leg in figure 3!

TURN-IN DRILL

Move to the sit-out position *(figures 1-5;
continued on next page)*.

1

2

3

4

5

TURN-IN DRILL
CONTINUED

Turn on your elbow and step your leg under your knee to complete the drill *(figures 6-9)*.

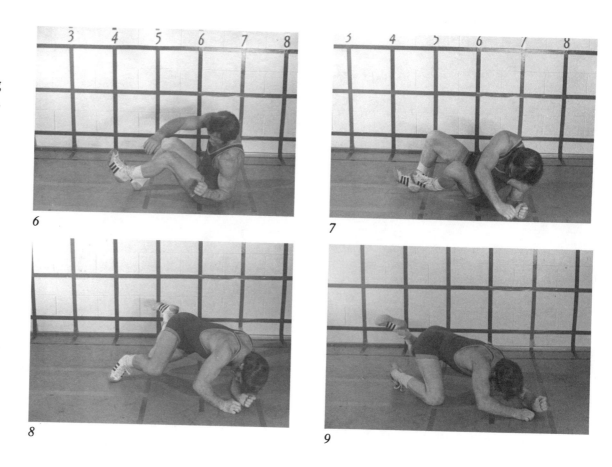

6

7

8

9

TURN-IN

Control your opponent's hand (*figures 1-3*) and force down with your thumbs (*figure 4*). Lean back, placing your head on his shoulder. Scoot away and turn-in to break free (*figures 5-7*).

The footwork is illustrated on the previous page (figures 7 and 8).

1

2

3

4

5

6

7

HEAD ROLL

From the sit position, control your opponent's wrist *(figure 1)*, catch his head and pull it over your shoulder *(figures 2-4)*. Turn to your side to finish *(figures 5-7)*.

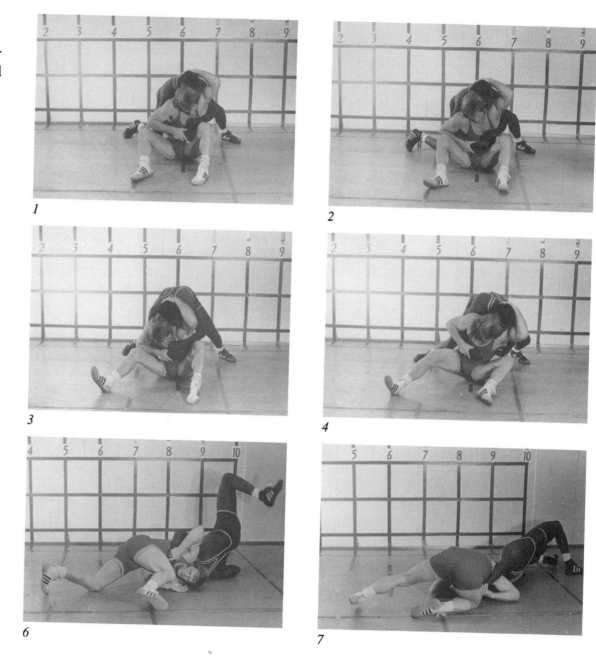

1

2

3

4

6

7

UNDERHOOK ARM LIFT

From the sit position, control your opponent's wrist, underhook his arm, and pull the arm over your head (*figures 1-4; continued on next page*).

The hip heist helps you complete the hold.

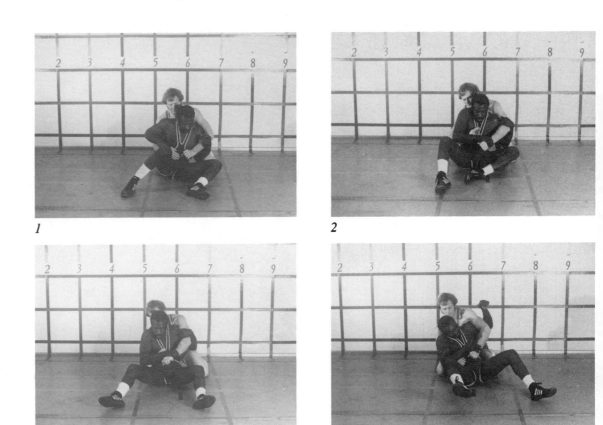

1

2

2

4

UNDERHOOK ARM LIFT
CONTINUED

Lean back and drop your shoulder to the mat. Reach around the waist and raise your head. Drive into him for the reversal (*figures 5-8*).

5

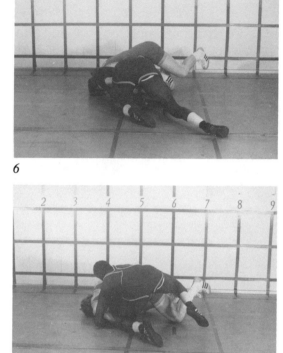

6

7

8

ARM DRAG

From the sit position, control your opponent's wrist *(figures 1-3)*. As he reaches over your shoulder, catch his arm, drive backwards, then scoot away, pulling his arm behind you. Move behind him for the reversal *(figures 4 and 5)*.

1

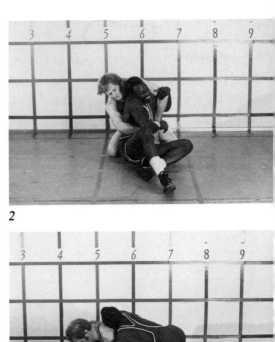

2

3

4

5

TURN-OUT DRILL

Jump to a side position on your right shoulder *(figures 1-4).* Turn to your knees, facing the opposite direction to complete the drill *(figures 5 and 6).*

1

2

3

4

5

6

TURN-OUT

Jump to a sit-out position, turn on your outside shoulder and swing your elbow down, knocking your opponent's arm off your waist.

1

2

3

4

5

TURN-OUT

HAND CONTROL

Move to a sit position and control your opponent's wrist *(figures 1-6; continued on next page).*

Note the back pressure (figures 1 and 2), and the hand control (figures 6-11).

1

2

3

4

5

6

TURN-OUT

HAND CONTROL, CONTINUED

Force down with your thumbs, lean back, and scoot away; turn on your elbow to escape (*figures 7-14*).

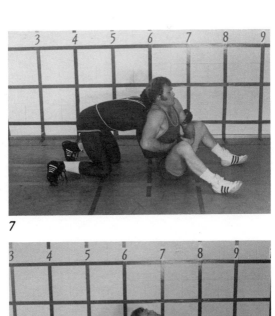

7

8

9

10

11

12

13

14

HEAD BLOCK

When your opponent places his head over your shoulder, catch his wrist and push his head back *(figures 1-3)*. Raise your hips and place your hand on the mat; step your leg under your knee, and turn to a face-off position *(figures 4 and 5)*.

Figures 1 and 2 show the hand and hip positions for the head-block sit-out. You can also grab your opponent's head and pull it over your shoulder or head!

1

2

3

4

5

SNAPBACK COUNTER

The bottom man attempts a sit-out. Under-hook his arm and pull back (*figures 1-3*). Use your chin to hold his shoulder (*figures 4-6*).

You should also try to grab your opponent's chin.

1

2

3

4

5

6

COUNTER

FOLLOW THE FEET

The bottom man attempts a sit-out and turn-in. Drive your chest into his back *(figures 1-4)*. Move toward his feet; stay behind his elbow, hips and legs for control *(figures 5-6). This is a good movement and conditioning drill!*

Note the position of Anderson's left hand in figure 4. This helps you move behind.

Figure 6 shows good top position.

1

2

3

4

5

6

COUNTER

REVERSE DIRECTION DRILL

The bottom man sits out and turns on his shoulder *(figures 1-3)*. Hook his elbow and pull down. Jump over the arm and catch him to regain control *(figures 4-6)*.

Stay off both knees as you move. Straddle the near leg. Keep your knee behind your opponent's hip and drive him forward (figure 7).

1

2

3

4

5

6

7

SIDE ROLL

From the bottom position, control your opponent's wrist. Swing your outside leg under your knee and sit to your side and elbow *(figures 1-5; continued on next page).*

The trick is to use your knees and feet like an extra pair of arms to elevate your opponent's legs and hips. Always create a perpendicular position to his body.

1

2

3

4

SIDE ROLL
CONTINUED

Pull down, sit into him and pull him over your back for the reversal *(figures 5-9)*.

Tip: Combine the roll with the switch and sit-out. Chain them together as one hold that changes into another depending on the position you find yourself in.

5

6

7

8

9

KNEE HOOK

From the bottom position, hook your foot behind your opponent's knee *(figures 1 and 2)*. Catch his wrist and sit into him. Drop to your elbow *(figures 3-5)*. Pull him over your back to finish *(figures 6 and 7; continued on next page)*.

1

2

3

4

5

6

7

KNEE HOOK
CONTINUED

8

9

10

Note how the foot pulls the knee to the mat (figures 8 and 9). Figure 10 shows the hip position.

FAKE STAND-UP

From the bottom position, start the outside leg stand-up *(figures 1-6)*. As your opponent drives you forward, catch his wrist and sit into him. Drop to your elbow and pull him over your back *(figures 7 and 8)*.

1

2

3

4

5

6

7

8

THIGH BLOCK

The execution is the same as that for the Fake Stand-up *(previous page)*.

Note the foot position in figure 4.

1

2

3

4

5

6

7

8

FOUR-POINT STANCE

The top man drives you forward *(figures 1-5)*. Move to all fours *(figure 6; continued on next page)*.

1

2

3

4

5

6

FOUR-POINT STANCE
CONTINUED

The top man hooks your leg and tries to pull you down on the mat. (*Continued on next page*).

Note the top man's knee position (figures 6 and 7). This is a good position from which to drill.

7

8

9

10

11

12

FOUR-POINT STANCE
CONTINUED

Catch his wrist and sit into him. Lift your
leg and pull him over your back to finish
(figures 13-19).

*Use the back of your free
hand to push your oppo-
nent's leg (figure 17).*

13

14

15

16

17

18

19

LEG HOOK

When the top man overhooks your leg, dip your inside hip to pull your leg free (*figures 1-4*). Move to a sit position (*figures 5 and 6; continued on next page*).

It's important to move into your opponent.

1

2

3

4

5

6

LEG HOOK
CONTINUED

Roll across your shoulders to score *(figures 7-11)*.

7

8

It's important to keep your chin tucked into your chest and use your legs in a cartwheel motion.

9

10

11

FAR-ARM SIDE ROLL

From a four-point position, reach across and catch your opponent's wrist, sit under his body and pull him over your back *(figures 1-4)*.

Hook your opponent's ankle with your foot and turn your knee into his body (figure 3).

1

2

3

4

ROLL COUNTER
KNEE HOOK AND HALF NELSON

The top man attempts a roll *(figures 1-3)*. Counter by underhooking his knee with your toe. Lift his leg and drive forward. Reach behind his head to regain control *(figures 4-8)*.

1

2

3

4

5

6

7

8

SIDE ROLL DRILL

From the bottom position, move to a side and elbow position *(figures 1-4)*. Return to your base *(figure 5; continued on next page)*.

As you do this drill without a partner, visualize what you're doing with your hip and why. Repeat until you can go full speed. Then get a partner and do repetitions at one-quarter speed, one-half speed, etc. Have him do the counter without blocking or stopping your movement. Chain this hold together with the switch and sit-out.

1

2

3

4

5

SIDE ROLL DRILL
CONTINUED

Change to the opposite hip and elbow to complete the drill *(figures 6-11)*.

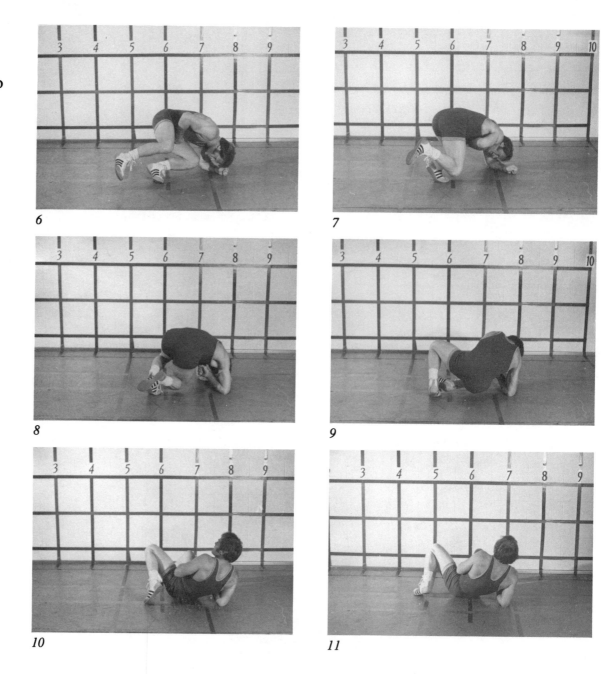

6

7

8

9

10

11

Ben Peterson switching

SWITCH

Move forward on your hands; swing your inside knee under your leg to the sit position *(figures 1-3)*. Scoot away as you reach inside the crotch. Grab the back crotch and pull yourself on top for the reversal *(figures 4-8)*.

1

2

3

4

5

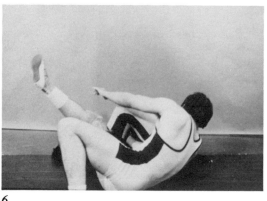

6

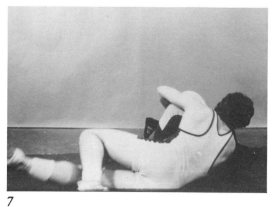

7

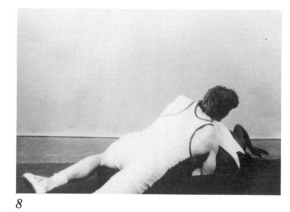

8

SWITCH REVERSAL

Move to all fours. Sit parallel to your opponent, reach inside the crotch and turn to the top position *(figures 1-5)*.

This is a good standing technique when your opponent is trying to break you down from behind or right after a takedown.

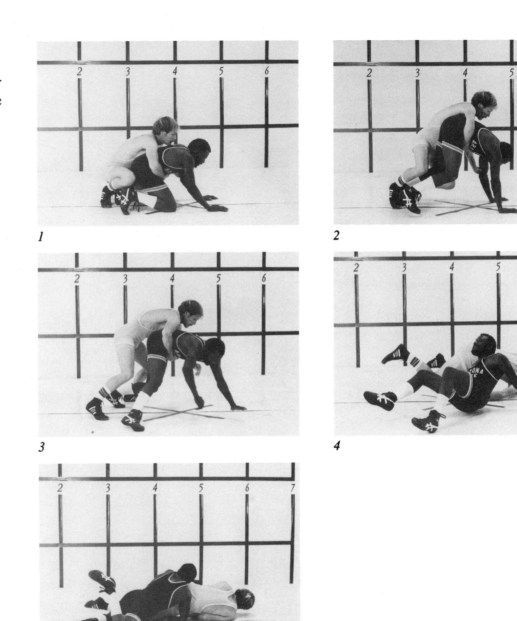

1

2

3

4

5

SIT-OUT

From the bottom, move to the sit position *(figures 1-3)*. Reach inside your opponent's crotch and move behind him to finish *(figures 4-6)*.

You need to scoot away and apply pressure against your opponent's arm to complete this hold.

Caution: Anytime you place your arm around the waist on the switch, you are in danger of the roll (figure 5).

1

2

3

4

5

6

UNDERHOOK

When the bottom man attempts a switch *(figures 1-3)*, underhook his arm and pull down *(figures 4-6)*. Move behind him and drive his head down *(figures 7 and 8)*.

1

2

3

4

5

6

7

8

SHOULDER DRIVE

The bottom man starts a switch *(figures 1-4)*. Move your leg away and drive your shoulder into his side, forcing him to the mat. Stay on your toes and behind his hips to maintain control *(figures 5 and 6)*.

Figure 1 shows good hand and feet position to start the switch.

Note the position of the knee in figure 6. This is a good top position.

1

2

3

4

5

6

SIT-THROUGH

The bottom man attempts a switch *(figures 1-3)*. Catch his thigh and sit behind him. Drop your shoulder on his arm and move to your knees to regain control *(figures 4-7)*.

1

2

Note figure 6: Position your knee between your opponent's legs to prevent the step-over (see next page).

3

4

5

6

7

ARM HOOK STEP-OVER

FRONT VIEW

The bottom man attempts a switch (*figures 1-3*). Catch his arm and swing your inside knee across his chest (*figures 4-6*).

Note the position of the head on the mat (figure 4).

1

2

3

4

5

6

STEP-OVER

REAR VIEW

The bottom man attempts a switch *(figures 1-3)*. Hook his arm and roll across your shoulder. Step across his body with your inside leg *(figures 4-9; continued on next page)*.

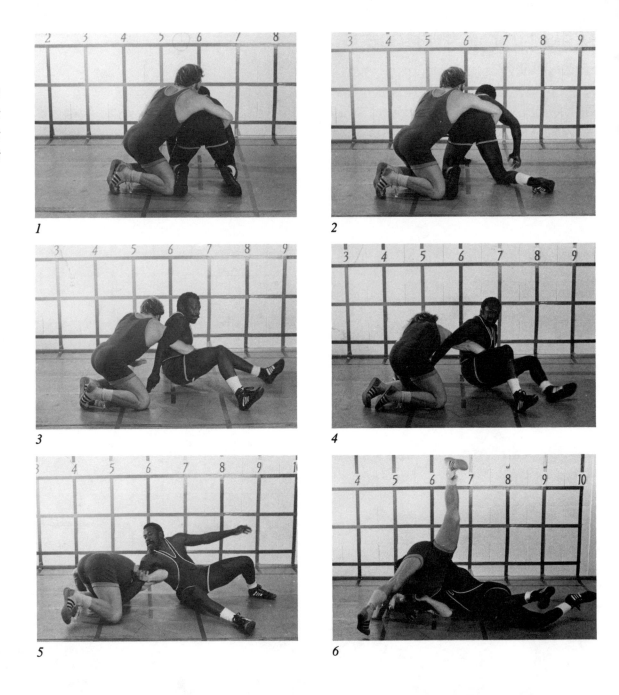

1

2

3

4

5

6

STEP-OVER
REAR VIEW, CONTINUED

7

8

9

The step is with the inside leg. Try for the pin when using this hold.

Fred Lett

1968 AAU Wrestling Championship - Bobby Douglas vs. Tom Huff

ARM HOOK AND STEP-OVER

The top man attempts a far-arm breakdown (*figure 1*). Catch his arm and pull it down (*figures 2-3*). Swing your inside leg across his chest (*figures 4-6*).

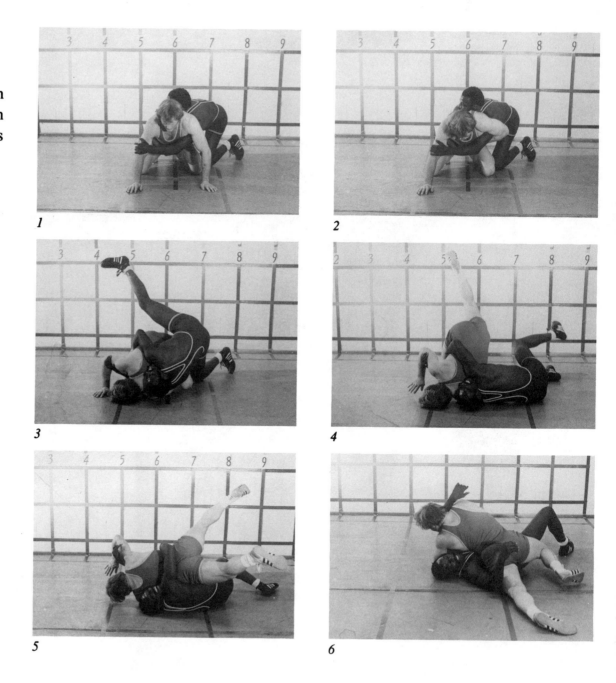

1

2

3

4

5

6

ARM HOOK

HALF NELSON OR CROSSFACE

The top man attempts a half nelson *(figures 1 and 2)* or a crossface *(figures 3 and 4)*. Pull forward and drive into him. Pull his shoulder to the mat and swing your legs over his body to score *(figures 5 and 6)*.

1

2

3

4

5

6

ARM HOOK

HIGH LEG OVER

The top man catches your ankle and reaches for your far arm *(figures 1-3)*. Hook his arm and pull down. Roll over your shoulders to a sit position on his chest. Cover his body for the pin *(figures 4-6)*.

1

2

3

4

5

6

FAKE SWITCH TURN-IN

From the bottom position, move as if you are going to switch *(figure 1)*. As your opponent moves away, drop to your elbow and sit your leg through *(figure 2)*. Turn on your shoulder to escape *(figures 3-4)*.

1

2

3

4

Be ready to move in for the takedown (figure 4).

WHIZZER FACE-OFF

From the bottom position, raise your outside leg. Swing your inside arm over your opponent's head and hook the arm *(figures 1-4)*. Pull him forward and across your body, and lift his leg with your leg *(figures 5 and 6; continued on next page)*.

Be ready to move behind your opponent when you face off.

1

2

3

4

5

6

WHIZZER FACE-OFF
CONTINUED

Sit away, place your hand on his head and face off *(figures 7-9)*.

7

8

9

Key points:
1. *Keep your head up.*
2. *Hold his arm tight.*
3. *Apply pressure down and forward at all times.*

COACH'S NOTES

I kept diaries throughout my wrestling career so that when I became a coach I'd have a map to follow. Little did I know how valuable those diaries would become.

The following training ideas are from my notes, collected from many of the great coaches and wrestlers whom I've had the honor of associating with. I hope they serve you well.

Bobby Douglas

Bobby Douglas (left), Phil Niekro and Coach George Kovalick

THE WILL TO WIN

It has been said, "The will to win is worthless without the will to prepare."

WRESTLING: THE PATH TO THE TOP

The ancient art of amateur wrestling is a sport of the highest order. Its major emphases are clean living and superb physical conditioning. Wrestling is known for its ability to develop an individual's skills to act and react intelligently in stressful situations. Wrestling aids in the development of valuable qualities and traits that will last an individual a lifetime.

A wrestler's goal should be to obtain a college education. Planning, studying and managing your time are keys to success. Academics are important to wrestlers. In the United States, the majority of all National, World and Olympic champions have attended colleges or universities.

Prospective college wrestlers should be aware of the importance that is being placed on academics. How the high school wrestler performs academically and competitively will determine his chance to obtain a college scholarship. To become a champion you must continue in school.

Torrae Jackson (back points)

FITNESS

No athlete is more fit than a wrestler. Wrestling is a sport that starts with boys and turns them into men.

Wrestling is very much like life: you reap what you sow. To be a champion, you have to pay the price: the miles on the track, the hours in the workout room, the pounds of sweat, the pain, the torture and the agonies of this slavery. You cannot win by just doing what is required during practice sessions. You have to work extra—running, weight training, drilling, studying films, etc. After wrestling, other things in life become easy.

Although the only way to learn to wrestle is by wrestling, you must also read about and study new methods. Keep up with new holds. Talk to others about their training.

Every wrestler wants to be a champion. The champion is willing to do the extras that are necessary to place him ahead of the rest.

PREVENTING INJURIES

Preventing injuries is one of the major concerns of coaches. Injuries cause a break in the training load and set students back on their timetables.

Injuries in wrestling occur within microseconds and most often when a wrestler is tired. Many injuries occur on contact with the mat or when limbs are taken beyond the range of motion (e.g., a bent leg, a shoulder or elbow forced too far).

There are some positions that are dangerous if you get into them. Sometimes it is better to lose the points than to lose the ankle, knee or shoulder. You have to make that choice and have little time in which to do it.

Incorrect executions of techniques also cause injuries:

- collision type: head butts account for about thirty percent of injuries.
- twisting type: these occur as a result of limbs being taken beyond their range of motion.
- other injuries are a combination of these two: e.g., head-on collision or finger in the eye, back trips or throws.

Practice safety; watch for hazards in various positions and holds. Most wrestlers will sustain a number of injuries during their careers. Knowing how to avoid injuries will determine how successful you can become.

Wrestlers must learn to react correctly to avoid injuries. They should learn the proper method of falling to prevent injuries from takedowns or counters. Contact with the mat accounts for the largest percentage of injuries.

Developing your conditioning, strength, and flexibility will help you avoid injuries.

STRETCHING AND FLEXIBILITY

Stretch before and after any workout.

Stretching is not a competitive effort; each individual has his own level of flexibility. Stretching is for self-improvement. Each athlete should be working solely to improve his own ability.

1. Always relax as you stretch.
2. Breathe normally as you stretch.
3. Do not stretch to a point at which you feel pain.
4. Never compare yourself with someone else regarding flexibility.
5. Never bounce as you stretch.
6. Stretch your tightest side first.
7. Stretch as often as possible.

Pay particular attention to # 5; do not bounce during stretching. This is dangerous, and an athlete who does this rather than completing a smooth and gradual movement is risking injury. The bounce actually forces the muscle to tighten in an effort to protect itself. Eventually, the forced motion can result in a muscle injury.

Flexibility comes with time; as in all areas of conditioning, a consistent effort is necessary. It is important to stretch often and certainly before practice and after competition.

ENDURANCE PROGRAM

The long-distance phase. Running a long distance at seven to nine m.p.h. (about an eight-minute mile) will raise the heartbeat rate to about 150 beats per minute. The heart must reach this level for at least 15 minutes for any positive improvement in endurance. This type of training should be done on alternate days on a soft surface to prevent shin splints and foot injuries.

A stronger heart will be able to pump blood to the muscles faster; therefore, oxygen will be delivered to fuel the muscles and waste material will be eliminated from tissue more rapidly.

The long-distance phase should cover the first four weeks of a conditioning program or preseason workout.

The jog and stride phase. The second stage of the endurance program requires alternate jogging and striding over a long distance without a rest period. This kind of training is done over two to three miles with he athlete doing alternate stages of jogging 200 yards and striding 200 yards. The important point is that there is no rest period over the entire distance.

As your heart becomes stronger, more oxygen will be transferred through the blood system into the muscles. This will help prevent early fatigue. As your mind adapts to an increased workload, you will be able to ignore the discomforts that precede fatigue. Willingness to accept pain complements your efforts to sustain grueling activity.

The jog and stride sequence prepares your body for intense efforts after short recovery periods. You begin to train through the "pain threshold" and to develop mental toughness.

The interval training phase. The third stage of the endurance program is speed work at a given pace with a timed rest period. The athlete is required to run distances of 120-220 yards, with a rest period in the range of 30-90 seconds.

The duration of the rest period is crucial. Any rest period of less than 30 seconds does not allow the heart enough recovery time. A rest period of more than 90 seconds is too long, since it allows the heart rate to drop sufficiently to prevent any endurance gains.

GRADUATED TRAINING, LOADING

With running, sparring, and weights, you can increase distance, time, and pounds. These increases will force your body to strengthen both physically and mentally, so that your overall performance will improve. As the demands increase, your body's ability to do harder work increases.

If you are to excel, your body must be pushed to the brink on occasion. As your internal alarm goes off and your body begins to set off its defensive mechanisms, persevere! It is at this point that most of the pain will come, and you need to push to the point of exhaustion.

The final phase.
1. Increase the intensity of the work (e.g., speed).
2. Increase the length of the work (e.g., distance).
3. Increase the number of attempts (e.g., repetitions).
4. Decrease the recovery time (e.g., rest).
5. Add to workload during recovery (e.g., exercise, jump rope).

There is no easy way of conditioning. The best conditioner for a wrestler is, of course, wrestling itself, but wrestling is not enough. The heart has to be developed, and your conditioning will be greatly aided by

supplementing your training with weight lifting, dancing, running, swimming, gymnastics, soccer, basketball, handball, and other sports and activities.

Be aware that our physical limitations are unknown, and in the sport of wrestling you must be willing to undergo great physical and mental stress. The mind is the final factor in all victories. Wrestlers must be able to think their way to victory. Pushing yourself farther than you thought you could go strengthens your ability to concentrate beyond pain. This intense preparation prepares you to be a champion.

STRENGTH TRAINING

Strength is the easiest area of conditioning to improve, yet it is probably the area that requires the most self-discipline. There are no secrets to weight training: the athlete who trains most consistently and works hardest improves the most.

The off-season is the best time for improving strength. This is the time when the wrestler can get the maximum gain, since he is not concentrating on wrestling.

The wrestler must deal realistically with the off-season. Very likely he will be working a job or attending school, or both. Thus he must discipline himself to insure he sets aside enough time for proper workout sessions. Normally, an athlete must spend at least one hour and fifteen minutes three times per week to make any significant gains in his strength. Remember, a stronger wrestler becomes a better wrestler.

When one muscle group (of a pair) contracts, the opposing muscle group (of a pair) lengthens, and vice versa. To reduce the possibility of injury, it is very important that an athlete exercise both muscle groups (of a pair). When one group of an antagonistic pair becomes disproportionately stronger, the likelihood that the weaker muscle group will suffer an injury (a pull, a sprain, a tear, etc.) is increased. Emphasize the lowering of the weight as well as the raising of the weight. When lifting, many athletes will concentrate on raising a weight, but once in the mid-range position of an exercise, they will *drop* the weight to return to the starting position for the exercise. Remember, the same muscles that raised the weight are the same muscles that will enable you to lower the weight. Do not circumvent half of the exercise.

I believe you can use your strength training program to increase your personal confidence, that deep-down residue of inner personal belief that allows ordinary people to achieve extraordinary accomplishments in every area of life. It comes from designing a program that allows you to make continual gains. It comes form setting realistic goals and working with intensity, dedication and perseverance to achieve them.

One of your objectives should be to organize a workout that will produce the maximum level of improvement in the least amount of time. A two-hour weight training workout is neither necessary nor productive. A three-set workout typically requires only approximately one hour to one and one half hours to complete, while a one-set workout takes a little less than one hour. A reasonable rest period between exercises is somewhere between thirty seconds and one minute. Any greater rest period can lead to a time-consuming, prolonged training session.

A set is the number of repetitions executed each time an exercise is performed. Like the controversy surrounding the question of how many repetitions should be performed in any set, there is a similar controversy over how many sets of any exercise should be performed. One theory recommends that only a single set be performed. The reasoning behind this theory is that one *properly performed* set will stimulate maximum gains in muscular strength and mass. If an athlete properly performs one set, he will certainly not want to perform a second set; and if he were to perform additional exercise, it could eventually become counter-productive. According to this theory, if a second set is performed, it is obvious that the first set was not properly performed.

WHAT ABOUT STRENGTH AND POWER?

When a wrestler is required to use his muscles, he often forgets to use his head. Strength and power without speed, timing, and position are useless.

THE WEIGHTS

Weight programs are a great value. Free weights serve the wrestler better because of the balance factor. When lifting in wrestling, you need to be able to shift your position several times before you can get into the proper position. With the free weights, you can get a better sense of the correct timing along with the strength and balance that are required. I do not believe in lifting heavy weights.

After I started lifting weights, I could feel additional strength playing a role when

I had to finish from a tough position or adjust to a mistake. It would not take as much energy or time; lifting helped my confidence. If you are a good wrestler, and you are trying to get better, the weights will definitely help! If you are injured and have limited time, the weights can make a difference in your rehabilitation and give you the strength to compensate for your injury. Weights allow you to get a workout even when you are injured. I scored many more takedowns after I started lifting.

INTENSITY

Emphasize intensity in your conditioning workouts. Maximum gains will not occur unless an athlete works at maximum intensity. *Exercise* through the full range of movement. If an athlete does not perform every exercise through the full range of movement, he eventually will lose flexibility in the joint areas, as well as fail to develop muscular fitness through the full range of movement. He will also be more prone to injury.

Exercise antagonistic muscle groups. Within the body, there are four major antagonistic (opposing) muscle groups.

    chest/lats
    biceps/triceps
    abdominals/lower back
    quads/hamstrings

Whenever possible, the athlete should exercise the potentially larger and stronger muscles of the body first. The athlete should progress from the muscles of the legs, to the torso, to the arms, to the abdominals, and finish with the muscles of the neck.

A workout program should be performed three days a week with adequate rest between individual workouts. The first couple of workouts concentrate on form and balance in the squat snatch, dead lifting more with your legs than your back, rolling your shoulders back at the top of your lift. Do only three sets of nine repetitions, even though you feel you can do more. On the next or subsequent workouts, do the first two sets of nine, the last two of ten; then three sets of ten; then two of ten and one of eleven and so on.

When you can do three sets of 11, move to four sets of nine. This way your goal is one more rep at a time, or one more set, the biggest jump being three reps, i.e., $3 \times 11 = 33$, $4 \times 9 = 36$. When you can do four sets of 11, increase the weight by 5% and drop back to three sets of 9. This way you can achieve a positive, realistic gain every time; plus, you only have to work on one exercise at a time, so the potential for gain is always there.

When you finish your last set of dead lifts, take a couple of old-fashioned plates, the kind without the grooves, and carry them for as long as you can, pinching them in your hands. See what a combination of dead lifting and carrying a plate does for your grip. Incidentally, when you do the dead lifts, keep both hands facing the same way. It will help your grip because the bar can more easily roll out of your hands.

Another factor to work against is time. Be concerned about it. Work slowly at first, but as you train, know how long a complete workout takes and then work to beat it. Start your weight training program in this manner. As you get into your program, keep a record of the total amount of weights you have lifted within a given time.

Each morning upon awakening, record your pulse (the lower the better). This will help make you more conscious of your physical condition. It can also be an indicator when something is wrong. If your pulse suddenly jumps up several points, it may mean that you have not fully recovered from the previous day's efforts, that you did not get enough rest, or that your body is fighting off an infection. In any case, it is a sign to back off; let your body recover before continuing to train hard.

TRAINING AIDS

Rope-climbing develops the pulling muscles, such as the arms, abdomen, back, and related shoulder muscles. It also increases strength of grip and mental fortitude. (Climb five to 10 times a day.)

Skipping rope is tremendously beneficial, aerobically, for any wrestler. Do it two ways: first, against the clock—three, six, twelve minutes; then count—the more jumps within a given time the greater the intensity.

LEADERSHIP

Leadership is the quality that is responsible for people following an individual, having faith in his judgment and abilities and being willing to work under his direction. A leader is someone who can accomplish something others would not attempt. Not everyone can hold an office such as President or Vice President, yet all can develop the qualities of good leadership.

COMMAND THE RESPECT OF OTHERS WHEREVER YOU ARE, IN WHATEVER YOU ARE DOING.

Study yourself. Discover your strong points and your weak points.

Study the personal qualities of effective coaching.

Endeavor to develop the qualities that will win the confidence of others, such as sound judgment, open-mindedness, freedom from prejudice, coolness in trying situations, sincerity, and *honesty.*

When a wrestler deserves credit for achievement—compliment him.

Admit mistakes and avoid excuses.

Be firm when ideals, principles or goals are at stake, but try not to give offense.

Refrain from hurting others' feelings unnecessarily.

Have facts before you reach a conclusion. *Develop good judgment.*

Plan to accomplish goals. Keep out of the limelight.

The more difficult the obstacle, the stronger one becomes after hurdling it.

WRESTLERS MUST DEVELOP THESE WINNING TRAITS:

Loyalty, to yourself and to all those dependent upon you. Keep your self-respect.

Cooperation, with all your coworkers. Help others see the other side.

Enthusiasm. Your heart must be in your work. Stimulate others. *Sacrifice personal gain for the benefit of the team.*

DEVELOP YOUR PERSONALITY:

- Through people you see, observe and have contact with.
- Through your associates.
- Through things you read and see.
- Through places you go and things you do.
- Through your environment.

ALWAYS CONDUCT SELF ANALYSIS

Am I easily discouraged?

Do I recognize and admit my mistakes?

Am I loyal to wrestling and its educational goals?

Can I make a decision quickly and accurately?

Can I accept honors and still keep my feet on the ground?

Am I following a plan of improvement and advancement?

Do I have religious convictions?

Do I have a definite aim in life?

Am I honest?

Am I playing the game of life fairly and

honestly with myself, my family and others?

HAVE YOUR HEART AND SOUL IN YOUR WORK

The desire to excel requires the ability to make decisions and think alone, the ability to resist temptation and stay with your cause, and the ability to concentrate on your objectives and be determined to reach your goal! This requires careful planning.

Continually think and plan ways to improve.

Coaching is a characteristic or trait that is not inherited but has to be developed in individuals. It is a series of abilities, characteristics and attitudes, generally evolving from experience. No one can make you a good coach- they can only point the way. You must make the transition.

HAVE A PLAN

When you try a hold that does not work or is blocked, switch to something else. It is generally useless to try to force a hold that is blocked; hence time, effort and energy are wasted.

The ability to analyze and predict situations before they happen, then to counterattack, plays a major role in winning.

Don't attempt things in a match that you have not made a sound part of your plan in practice.

Be cool and collected in all situations. Never quit! It is difficult for an opponent to get full control of you if you are in rapid continuous motion.

Don't stop before you hear the referee's whistle. Don't complain to the official. Don't stop the clock by going off the mat needlessly when you are ahead and the time is running out. It is wrong to ease up because your opponent has done so or because you anticipate he will so.

Learn offense, since defense is more natural and comes more easily to most wrestlers.

Chain wrestling is essential to success in wrestling. Learn holds in meaningful relation to other holds, not as isolated maneuvers.

Use holds that have a good calculated risk. Determine what can happen to you if the hold fails to work properly. If there is even a remote possibility that you will end up on your back, don't do it!

Don't get into a rut by using just one or two holds at the expense of other fundamental holds.

The body has the unique ability to develop strength as you drill and wrestle. The more you work in positions that require strength and power, the stronger and more powerful you become. The faster you're able to complete a drill, the faster you'll be able to execute the hold.

COMMUNICATION-COACHES AND WRESTLERS PLAN TOGETHER

We can reach goals through communication. Only through communication can the coaching staff make wrestlers aware of desires, demands and expectations.

Although the only way learn to wrestle is by wrestling, wrestlers must also read about and study new methods.

Coaches, speak simply, clearly and plainly. Do not try to show off by using big words. Use short sentences, effective pauses. Listen to your wrestlers' opinions and responses; be positive.

Select the techniques that are most effective and will work against the main opponents.

APPENDIX A: WEIGHT LOSS DIET

MAKING WEIGHT
BY BOBBY DOUGLAS

My first experience with making weight was at Bridgeport High School my freshman year. I was the second team 103-pounder—my normal weight was 97 pounds. When the season started I could eat as much as I wanted and never needed to worry about making weight.

I had my first bad experience when on the day of weigh–ins I was three pounds over. Shedding those three pounds taught me the true meaning of wrestling. I had no idea that my weight would jump as high as it did, but I did know it would be tough taking it off. I'd never cut weight before because I was always two or three pounds under. The seniors told me what I had to do. They also told me what would happen if I didn't do it.

I learned about discipline when our heavyweight, Tiny, convinced me that if I didn't make weight, it would be a fate

worse than death. I remember the fear when the captain asked me about my weight. I said that I was down.

To make weight that day, I went to the furnace room of my high school, during the next hour and a half, I cut the three pounds. During that time I learned discipline. I felt I couldn't stop because my teammates were depending on me. I heard George Kovalick's words about courage. I felt the fear of failure, and I knew that making weight was part of the spirit of wrestling. It was during that time I really became a wrestler.

RECOMMENDED DIET FOR WEIGHT LOSS, WRESTLING ATHLETES
BY KAREN MOSES

The following diet was planned to ensure adequate vitamins, minerals, carbohydrates and protein while limiting calories for weight loss. The 1900-calorie sample diet provides adequate amounts of most nutrients for a male, age 19 to 22. The nutrient zinc is present at only 80% of the Recommended Dietary Allowance (RDA); thus it is advised that a multi-vitamin/mineral tablet containing 100% of the RDA for zinc be

taken two to three times per week. The higher calorie diets contain at least 100% of all essential nutrients. Protein in the diets meets the RDA for protein of a 290-pound man. Dietary carbohydrate provides greater than 60% of the calories, which is suggested for athletes in order to supply the body with adequate glycogen for energy. Calories in the diet are reduced through limiting the use of fats and oils.

It is very important when losing weight that the athlete lose excess fat instead of valuable body fluids, muscle or organ protein. To prevent the wasting away of lean body mass during weight loss, an athlete should lose only one to two pounds per week. Weight loss techniques such as sweat baths, fasting, vomiting, using laxatives or diuretics or denying the body fluids may produce rapid weight loss. However, these weight loss techniques result in body water loss and muscle loss and hurt athletic performance. As a wrestler, it is important to keep weight at or near performance weight. If weight stays within five to ten pounds of performance weight, an athlete should be able to lose that weight in three to five weeks without using weight loss techniques that can harm athletic performance.

The 1900-calorie weight loss plan described in this text may be too low in calories for some athletes. Instructions on how to estimate caloric need are included below. Athletes whose calorie need is greater than 1900 should add additional calories according to the instructions in the section "Meal Plan for Higher Calorie Diets."

Keep in mind that each body is different. If you find that you are losing weight too quickly or too slowly, that you are tired or weak, or even that you don't like any of the food choices offered—speak up! Your coach, doctor and/or nutritionist can design a weight loss diet that more specifically meets your needs.

After you have lost the necessary amount of weight, continue eating a well-balanced, high-carbohydrate diet. This will help you to maintain your performance weight.

NUTRITION GUIDELINES

1. When possible, choose low-fat or non-fat products such as light cream cheese, light mayonnaise, 1% or skim milk.
2. Avoid cheese, nuts and fatty meats. All are high-fat items and add extra calories even in small portions.
3. Cut back on fried foods. Meats that are boiled, broiled, or grilled and vegetables that are boiled or steamed are better choices.
4. Remove the skin before eating chicken or turkey.
5. Use water-packed tuna.
6. Eat at least one dark green or yellow/orange vegetable every day, e.g., spinach, carrots, and tomatoes.
7. Eat a food that is a good source of vitamin C every day, e.g., orange juice, citrus fruit, kiwi, strawberries, grapefruit, bell peppers, broccoli, tomatoes.
8. Drink plenty of water.
9. Cut back on the amount of fats you add to foods, e.g., butter, margarine, mayonnaise, sour cream, regular salad dressing.
10. Eat foods that are high in complex carbohydrates often. This includes starchy vegetables, legumes (beans and peas), breads, cereals and other grain foods.

EATING BEFORE AN EVENT (MATCH OR PRACTICE)

1. Eat three to four hours before an event to make sure the stomach has time to empty and to help prevent cramping.
2. Pre-event meals should be high in carbohydrates. Sample meals include:
   - orange juice, corn flakes, banana, whole wheat toast with jelly and skim milk
   - vegetable soup, sliced turkey sandwich on wheat bread, fruit and low-fat strawberry yogurt
   - vegetable salad topped with lean ham, low-fat salad dressing, hard roll and skim milk
   - pasta with tomato sauce, Italian bread and small vegetable salad with low-fat dressing
3. Pre-event meals should not be high in fat or protein, as these nutrients slow digestion. Foods to avoid include:
   - hamburgers, hot dogs, cheese crisp, sausage, peanut butter
   - deep-fried or fried foods like doughnuts, french fries, hash browns, chips
   - condiments like mayonnaise, regular salad dressing, cream cheese, margarine or butter
4. A liquid meal can be taken up to one hour before an event. For example:
   - yogurt shakes
   - sports drinks
   - instant breakfast beverages
5. No food should be eaten less than one hour before an event. This can cause stomach upset or cramping, which can hurt performance. However, the athlete

should drink plenty of water or other dilute fluids during this time.

6. Within the first hour after training, replace lost carbohydrates (glycogen) with beverages, meals and snacks that are high in carbohydrates. This will aid recovery from a strenuous workout. High-carbohydrate items include:

- cereal, bread, pasta, muffins, pancakes, rolls and other grain foods
- fruit, fruit juice, dried fruit and vegetables, especially starchy vegetables like potatoes and corn
- milk, yogurt, cocoa, ice milk, milk shakes, ice cream and frozen yogurt—these foods can also be very high in fat, so choose the low-fat varieties
- legumes like refried beans, lima beans and chili beans

Other foods include:

- cakes, pies, cookies, and soft drinks—These foods get their carbohydrates from sugar and are often high in fat and low in nutrients. Supply carbohydrates by using the other carbohydrate sources listed above.
- Meat and cheese are low in carbohydrates, high in protein, and often high in fat.

HINTS FOR WEIGHT LOSS

1. Use the sample diets on the following pages as a guide for weight loss.
2. Fats are truly fattening, so it is especially important to avoid fried foods, fatty meats, cheese, whole milk and added fats like sour cream, mayonnaise, salad dressing, margarine and butter.
3. Stay away from sugary snacks like soda pop, candy and other sweets. These snacks can make your weight loss program backfire.
4. Drink lots of noncaloric beverages before and during a meal. Beverages like water, tea and diet pop will help fill you up without adding calories.
5. It takes your stomach about 20 minutes to tell your brain that it is no longer hungry. Eat a low-calorie snack about 20 minutes before a meal and, like your mother says, "You'll ruin your dinner." Low-calorie snacks include apples, oranges, grapes, carrots, lettuce, etc.
6. Another idea is to make the salad course last 20 minutes, or to eat slowly. It is common to eat two plates full of food before you realize you are no longer hungry.
7. Make sure you are not confusing hunger with thirst. You may think you are hungry when a glass of water would satisfy your craving.
8. Keep busy, within about 10 minutes your hunger pangs usually ease up.

DRINK WATER OR OTHER DILUTE FLUIDS

1. Drink plenty of dilute fluids before, during and after events and practice sessions. Commercial fluid replacement drinks contain a small amount of carbohydrate. Drinks like this will help maintain carbohydrate stores in the body. Stay away from fruit juice before and during workouts—it is high in natural sugars, which can cause stomach discomfort or, for some athletes, can cause a sugar rebound.
2. Drink about $2\frac{1}{2}$ cups of water or dilute fluids two hours before training.
3. Drink about 2 cups of fluid 10 to 15 minutes prior to training.
4. Drink about $\frac{1}{2}$ cup of fluid every 10 minutes, or $1\frac{1}{2}$ cups every 30 minutes, during an event or practice session.
5. After a workout, drink 2 cups for every one pound of body weight lost during training. (Two cups of water weighs one pound.)
6. Don't forget to drink or eat something

high in carbohydrates within one hour after training. This will aid recovery from the workout.

SAMPLE DIETS

The following sample diets can be used to achieve healthy weight loss. Keep in mind that it is never wise to lose more than one to two pounds per week. If you are following one of the sample diets and find you are losing weight too quickly, increase calorie amount as instructed.

WHICH DIET TO FOLLOW

In order to decide which diet to follow, you will need to know approximately how many calories your body needs each day to maintain weight. The formula below will give you an estimate of your caloric needs.

FORMULA

Step One: Multiply your weight by 11.
Example: 200 lbs. x 11 = 2200
Step Two: Multiply the product by one of the following amounts, based on your activity level. This will give a calorie range appropriate for you.

Light	1.4 - 1.6
Moderate	1.6 - 1.8
Hard	1.8 - 2.0
Severe	2.0 - 2.8
Very Severe	3.0

Example: 2200 x 1.4 = 3088 calories
2200 x 1.6 = 3520 calories
Calorie range: 3088 to 3520 calories per day. Aim for about 3000 to 3500 calories per day.

Theoretically, 3500 calories is equal to a pound of fat. This means that by reducing the number of calories you eat by 500 per day, you may lose one pound per week. There are other factors that affect the rate of weight loss; however, use the above formula to estimate the calories you need for weight loss.

Once you calculate the number of calories you need, eat 500 to 1000 calories less than you need. This should result in a one- to two-pound weight loss each week.

Reminder: It is best to lose only one to two pounds per week. Otherwise, you may lose muscle along with or instead of fat. A 500- to 1000-calorie change in your diet should keep your weight loss within this range. If not, then switch to a lower or higher calorie diet. (Instructions for adding calories to the 1900-calorie plan appear on page 153.)

1900-CALORIE SIX-DAY MEAL PLAN

DAY 1

Breakfast:
  4 small pancakes
  ¼ cup syrup, low-calorie
  1 cup skim milk
Snack:
  1 orange
  ½ peanut butter sandwich made of:
    1 slice bread
    1 tsp. peanut butter
Lunch:
  turkey sandwich made of:
    3 slices turkey lunchmeat
    2 slices bread
    2 tsp. mustard
    lettuce and tomato
  vegetable salad made of:
    lettuce
    ¼ large tomato
    ¼ cup broccoli
    ¼ cup cucumber
    ¼ cup onion
    low-fat or non-oil salad dressing
Snack:
  1 cup nonfat plain yogurt mixed with ½
    cup fresh or canned peaches
Dinner:
  1 grilled or broiled chicken breast (no
    skin)
  1 cup broccoli
  ½ cup boiled potato
  1 roll
  vegetable salad (same as lunch salad)
  2 cups skim milk
Snack:
  4 cups air-popped popcorn
  1 cup orange juice

Substitute:
  4 small waffles or 4 slices toast
  2 Tbsp. regular syrup or jelly
  1 cup 1% milk

  ½ grapefruit, ½ cup orange juice, 1 cup
    strawberries, or 1 kiwi
  1 slice toast with 1 tsp. margarine and 1
    tsp. jelly

  chicken, ham, or lean roast beef may
    replace turkey

  spinach or other leafy vegetable
  bell pepper, carrot, cauliflower, cabbage,
    celery

  vinegar or lemon juice

  1 cup skim milk and ½ cup fresh or
    canned fruit

  2 chicken thighs (no skin) or 3 oz. tuna
    (water-packed)
  1 cup green or yellow vegetable
  ½ cup corn or peas
  1 slice bread
  vegetable salad (same as lunch salad)
  2 cups skim milk

  ½ cup pretzels
  1 cup juice

1900-CALORIE SIX-DAY MEAL PLAN

DAY 2

Breakfast:
    1$\frac{1}{2}$ cup corn flakes
    2 cups skim milk
    1 banana
Snack:
    1 apple
Lunch:
    tuna sandwich made of:
        3 oz. tuna (water-packed)
        2 slices bread
        celery and onion (optional)
        2 tsp. low-fat mayonnaise
    1 small bowl of broth-based soup (e.g.,
        chicken noodle)
Snack:
    $\frac{1}{2}$ bagel
Dinner:
    spaghetti made with:
        2 cups spaghetti noodles
        $\frac{1}{2}$ cup tomato sauce
        $\frac{1}{4}$ cup ground beef
        1 Tbsp. Parmesan cheese
    vegetable salad (as in Day 1)
Snack:
    1 cup plain nonfat yogurt
    1 cup fresh fruit

Substitute:
    1$\frac{1}{2}$ cup cereal
    2 cups skim milk
    1 apple or orange

1 fruit

3 oz. lean meat may replace tuna

1 small bowl of pea soup

2 slices bread or toast

Spanish rice made with:
    2 cups rice
    $\frac{1}{2}$ cup salsa
    $\frac{1}{4}$ cup ground beef
    $\frac{1}{4}$ cup grated cheddar
1 cup cooked vegetables

1 cup skim milk
1 cup fresh fruit

1900-CALORIE SIX-DAY MEAL PLAN

DAY 3

Breakfast:
- 1 poached or hard-boiled egg
- 1 slice toast
- 1/2 grapefruit
- 2 cups skim milk

Snack:
- 1/2 bagel
- 1/2 Tbsp. low-fat cream cheese

Lunch:
- pasta salad made of:
  - 1 cup cooked pasta shells
  - 1 1/2 cups raw vegetables
  - 2 oz. chopped ham
  - 1/4 cup non-oil Italian dressing
- 1 roll

Snack:
- 1/2 banana
- 1 cup skim milk

Dinner:
- 2 bean burritos, each made of:
  - 1 small flour tortilla
  - 1/4 cup refried beans
  - 2 Tbsp. grated cheddar
  - 2 Tbsp. salsa
- 1/2 cup rice topped with salsa

Snack:
- 1 cup low-fat fruit-flavored yogurt

Substitute:
- 5 cooked egg whites
- 1/2 English muffin
- 1 orange
- 2 cups skim milk

- 2 slices toast
- 1 Tbsp. jelly

- spaghetti made of:
  - 1 1/2 cups spaghetti noodles
  - 1/2 cup tomato sauce
  - 2 oz. lean ground beef
  - 1 Tbsp. Parmesan cheese
- 1 slice bread

- 1 apple, orange or other fruit
- 1 cup nonfat yogurt

- 2 slices thin-crust cheese pizza

- vegetable salad (as in Day 1)

- 1 banana or other fruit

- 1 cup skim milk

1900-CALORIE SIX-DAY MEAL PLAN

DAY 4

Breakfast:

    2 slices toast

    2 tsp. jelly

    1/2 cup orange juice

    1 cup skim milk

Snack:

    1/2 bagel

Lunch:

    stir-fried vegetables made of:

        1 cup broccoli

        1 cup chopped cabbage

        1 Tbsp. soy sauce

        garlic and onion

    1 cup rice

    1 fruit

Snack:

    1 cup cereal

    1 cup skim milk

Dinner:

    4 oz. lean steak

    1 baked potato topped with cottage
        cheese

    spinach salad made with:

        spinach leaves

        mixed vegetables

        non-oil salad dressing

    1 small roll

Snack:

    4 graham crackers

    1 cup skim milk

Substitute:

    1 English muffin

    2 tsp. jelly

    1 orange or 1/2 grapefruit

    1 cup skim milk

    10-12 crackers

    1 cup other green vegetable

    1 cup other vegetable

    1 cup noodles

    1 fruit

    1 cup cereal

    1 cup skim milk

    4 oz. lean meat

    1 cup potato, corn or peas

    vegetable salad (as in Day 1)

    vinegar or lemon juice

    1 slice bread

    3 slices toast and jelly

    1 cup skim milk

1900-CALORIE SIX-DAY MEAL PLAN

DAY 5

Breakfast:
    1 cup cooked oatmeal
    1 cup skim milk
    1 orange
Snack:
    1 oz. pretzels
Lunch:
    ham sandwich made of:
        1 bun
        3 slices ham
        mustard
        tomato and lettuce
    1 fruit
    1 cup skim milk
Snack:
    1 small bran muffin
    1 cup skim milk
Dinner:
    tuna casserole made of:
        1 cup pasta
        3 oz. tuna (water-packed)
        1/2 cup nonfat plain yogurt
        1/4 tsp. garlic
        1/4 cup mushrooms
        1/4 cup onions
    1/2 cup peas
    1 small roll
    vegetable salad (as in Day 1)
Snack:
    6 cups air-popped popcorn
    1 cup orange juice

Substitute:
    2 cups cold cereal
    1 cup skim milk
    1/2 grapefruit

    3 cups popcorn (no oil or "Lite")

    other lean meat sandwich
        made the same way

    1 fruit
    1 cup skim milk

    1/2 bagel
    1 cup skim milk

    spaghetti made of:
        1 cup pasta
        3 oz. lean meat
        1/4 cup tomato sauce
        1/4 cup mushrooms
        1/4 cup onions

    1/2 cup corn or potatoes
    1 slice bread
    spinach salad (as in Day 4)

    2 oz. pretzels
    1 cup apple juice

1900-CALORIE SIX-DAY MEAL PLAN

DAY 6

Breakfast:
- 1 English muffin
- 2 tsp. jelly
- 1 cup skim milk
- 1 fruit

Snack:
- peanut butter sandwich made of:
    - 2 slices bread
    - 2 tsp. peanut butter

Lunch:
- ½ pkg. Ramen noodles mixed with:
    - 1½ cups broccoli
- 1 fruit

Snack:
- 2 fig newtons
- 2 cups skim milk

Dinner:
- 4 oz. baked/broiled fish
- ½ cup corn
- 1 cup carrots
- vegetable salad (as in Day 1)
- 1 small roll
- 1 orange

Snack:
- 1 cup cereal (corn flakes)
- 1 cup skim milk

Substitute:
- 2 slices toast
- 2 tsp. jelly
- 1 cup skim milk
- 1 fruit

- cheese sandwich made of:
    - 2 slices bread
    - 1 slice cheese

- pasta salad (as in Day 3)

- 1 fruit

- 2 cookies
- 2 cups skim milk

- 4 oz. lean meat
- ½ cup peas or potatoes
- 1 cup spinach
- spinach salad (as in Day 4)
- 1 slice bread
- 1 apple

Snack:
- 2 slices bread
- 1 cup skim milk

MEAL PLAN FOR HIGHER CALORIE DIETS

For each additional 500 calories needed, add one serving of food from each of the following lists:

One of:

    1 cup fruit juice

    1 banana

    1 large apple, pear or grapefruit

One of:

    1$\frac{1}{2}$ cup cold cereal

    1 cup hot cereal

    2 slices bread

    1 large flour tortilla

One of:

    $\frac{1}{2}$ cup potato

    $\frac{1}{2}$ cup rice

    $\frac{1}{2}$ cup pasta

    $\frac{1}{3}$ cup pinto beans

    1 cup milk

One of:

    2 oz. lean meat, fish or poultry

    1 oz. cheese

    $\frac{1}{2}$ cup cottage cheese

One of:

    $\frac{1}{2}$ cup cooked vegetable

    1 cup raw vegetable

For example: If you are losing weight at a rate of four pounds per week—that is two pounds per week more than the recommended rate of weight loss—you need to increase your calorie amount by 1000 calories per day. That means you need to choose two servings of food from *each* of these lists.

DIET ANALYSIS
AN EVALUATION OF THE 1900-CALORIE SIX-DAY MEAL PLAN

NUTRIENT	SUGGESTED VALUE	SIX-DAY AVERAGE	% RDA	SUPPLEMENTS = N					
				DAY 1	DAY 2	DAY 3	DAY 4	DAY 5	DAY 6
Calories (Kcals)	2900	1867.47		1751.89 0	1877.96 0	1930.14 0	1881.07 0	1863.97 0	1899.79 0
Fat (g)	***	27.29		25.36 0	19.28 0	34.93 0	26.67 0	24.48 0	33.00 0
Saturated fat (g)	***	8.21		7.06 1	6.55 1	14.46 1	9.49 1	24.48 0	33.00 0
Poly unsat fat (g)	***	2.99		3.77 7	2.26 7	4.18 7	1.64 6	6.37 1	5.33 2
Protein (g)	56	109.86		117.95 0	114.85 0	98.98 0	100.62 0	2.53 9	3.55 8
Carbohydrates (g)	***	305.53		271.60 0	317.81 0	309.96 0	318.15 0	119.84 0	106.91 0
Ethanol (g)	***	0.00		0.00 1	0.00 0	0.00 2	0.00 1	301.02 0	314.64 0
Fibre (g)	***	16.33		13.10 13	13.42 12	11.20 15	30.14 12	0.00 0	0.00 2
Cholesterol (mg)	***	177.51		178.53 1	139.23 0	364.01 1	109.25 0	17.92 14	12.23 14
Sodium (mg)	1100-3300	3556.67		3103.15 1	3873.74 0	4371.26 0	3118.93 0	159.95 1	114.09 2
Potassium (mg)	1875-5625	4689.71		4911.37 1	4561.98 0	4244.11 1	4555.17 0	3964.93 0	2908.00 0
P/S fat ratio	1.0	0.36		0.53	0.35	0.29	0.17	4513.16 0	4752.45 1
Carbo Kcal (%)	58.0	61.35		58.14	63.46	60.22	63.42	0.40	0.67
Fat Kcal (%)	30.0	13.59		13.46	9.55	16.83	13.19	60.56	62.11
Protein Kcal (%)	12.0	24.12		27.60	25.08	21.03	21.93	12.22	16.16
Alcohol Kcal (%)	***	0.00		0.00	0.00	0.00	0.00	26.36	23.07
Vit. A (IU)	5000	18468.42	369.37	16237.21 1	14319.54 0	5269.84 0	15665.38 0	0.00	0.00
Vit. E TOT-TOC (IU)	***	5.08	***	4.66 15	4.92 10	6.40 15	4.21 12	12850.53 1	46468.00 1
Vit. C (mg)	60	258.81	431.35	396.70 1	209.74 0	171.57 2	252.73 0	8.14 15	2.17 17
Thiamin-B1 (mg)	1.5	2.12	141.36	2.06 1	2.15 0	1.93 1	1.64 0	241.25 2	280.87 2
Ribo.-B2 (mg)	1.7	2.83	166.72	3.03 1	2.98 0	2.61 0	2.64 0	2.90 0	2.05 0
Niacin-B3 (mg)	19	24.79	130.49	26.82 1	36.25 0	14.02 1	19.35 0	2.68 0	3.06 0
Vit. B6 (mg)	2.2	2.59	117.78	2.24 5	3.10 2	2.06 1	2.61 1	31.39 0	20.92 0
Folate (mcg)	400	400.14	100.04	467.02 5	391.55 3	322.05 3	442.89 2	2.12 4	3.42 3
Vit. B12 (mcg)	3	6.27	209.02	5.79 6	7.22 3	5.21 4	5.71 3	350.31 5	427.03 5
Calcium (mg)	800	1634.74	204.34	1867.84 1	1455.11 0	1815.38 0	1348.63 0	6.50 5	7.20 5
Phosphorous (mg)	800	2014.66	251.83	2112.85 1	1920.50 0	1945.95 1	1717.84 0	1530.64 0	1790.87 0
Magnesium (mg)	350	459.76	131.36	479.49 4	417.03 3	404.13 1	459.88 1	2237.28 0	2153.55 1
Iron (mg)	10	15.95	159.50	13.18 1	18.25 0	13.39 1	17.57 0	449.65 2	548.39 3
Zinc (mg)	15	12.41	82.73	10.58 4	14.66 2	11.75 4	14.08 1	15.88 0	17.43 0
								14.20 1	9.19 3

APPENDIX B
MAJOR HIGH SCHOOL DIFFERENCES

The following material subject to annual review and change. Permission to reprint granted by NCAA.

	HIGH SCHOOL	COLLEGE
RIDING TIME	No riding time.	One point for one minute or more accumulated time advantage more than opponent.
FALL	Two seconds.	One second.
WEIGHT CLASSES	103, 112, 119, 125, 130, 135, 140, 145, 152, 160, 171, 189, 275.	118, 126, 134, 142, 150, 167, 177, 190, Heavyweight (177-275).
LENGTH OF MATCH	Three two-minute periods.	First period, three minutes; second and third periods, two minutes.
CONSOLATION MATCHES	Three periods: first, one minute; second and third, two minutes.	Three two-minute periods.
NUMBER OF MATCHES	No wrestler shall compete in more than five full-length matches in any day.	No similar rule.
WEIGHT ALLOWANCE	No allowance.	Three-pound allowance in November and December, 2 pounds in January, 1 pound in February, except qualifying tournaments, which are scratch weight.
WEIGH-IN	Shoulder-to-shoulder weigh-in within a maximum of one hour and a minimum of one-half hour before the time a dual meet is scheduled to begin.	Maximum of five hours and minimum of one-half hour, unless otherwise mutually agreed upon. (Contestant must face away from the dial or weight indicator of the scale.)

continued on next page

	HIGH SCHOOL	COLLEGE
COMPETITION	A wrestler weighing in for one weight class may be shifted to a higher weight, provided it is not more than one weight class above that for which his actual stripped weight qualifies him.	A contestant qualified to wrestle at one weight class may wrestle at any higher weight class except heavyweight.
SWEAT BOX	The use of a sweat box or similar heat devices for weight reduction purposes is prohibited. Rubber, vinyl and plastic suits also are prohibited.	No similar rule.
HEAVYWEIGHT CLASS	Unlimited-class contestants must weight a minimum of 184 pounds.	Contestants must weigh a minimum of 177 pounds.
ILLEGAL HOLDS	Any Salto or suplay in which a contestant goes to the top of his head from the standing position is illegal.	Straight back suplay and overscissors are illegal. Toe hold is potentially dangerous.
OVERTIME	Is extension of the regular match, with all penalties, warnings, cautions and injury time carrying over to overtime.	Is a new match, with warnings and penalties not cumulative from match to overtime period. Injury time does carry over. Criteria will determine winner if overtime ends in a draw.

APPENDIX C
ABOUT THE NEW OLYMPIC FREESTYLE RULES

The following is reprinted courtesy of Rick Tucci.

Match: The match remains at five minutes, with a minimum of three points needed to terminate the bout at five minutes. If three points are not achieved, the bout immediately goes into overtime for a maximum of three minutes. At the end of overtime, if three points have not been achieved, then criterion will be used to determine the winner.

If the score is 2-0, 2-1 or 1-0, generally the wrestler with the most points will be declared the winner. However, the entire match, including the overtime, is considered in declaring a winner. If the match remains tied, then the officiating team will meet and decide the winner.

Passivity is considered in all cases. Passivity can be given an unlimited amount of times to either wrestler. The passivity call (P) will be recorded on the scoresheet on the outside of the scoring column of the offended wrestler. When giving a passivity call, confirmation must be obtained and the opponent of the offended wrestler gets a choice of standing or putting his opponent in the par-terre position.

Par terre position: *For incorrect top position* (jumping forward and false starts): First time: friendly warning (attention); Second time: caution (same as caution for disqualification) - no point; Third and subsequent times: Caution and opponent will have choice in a change of position or standing

For incorrect bottom position: First time: friendly warning (attention); Second time: caution (same as caution for disqualification) - no point; Third and subsequent times: Caution and one point awarded to top wrestler. Same position.

Lift point: Lifting your opponent from the ground (par terre wrestling) which causes the wrestler to completely lose contact with the mat, and scores three or five points, will earn an extra point. The signal will be 3&1 or 5&1.

Escape point: This is a very touchy rule. When a bottom wrestler creates a move through effort after being dominated, he will earn one point.

Quick standups on the whistle, with no contact besides the hands or the back, will not earn a point. Cross ankle kickouts will not earn a point.

Only from a break in a hold, standing, facing your opponent, will earn the point. I know we will have a lot of questions and we hope to clear this up at our clinics.

Fleeing the hold: If a wrestler avoids contact and refuses to wrestle without fleeing the mat, a caution is given and one point is awarded to his opponent. Choice is given to the opponent of the offended wrestler. Problems will arise in distinguishing a passivity call (P) and a fleeing the hold call (O). Fleeing the mat and illegal hold calls remain the same (Caution and 1 or 2 and choice to opponent).

Classification system: 4-0 for Fall; 4-0 for 10-point difference when opponent has not scored; 4-1 for 10-point difference when opponent has scored; 3-1 for less than 10-point decision when loser scores; 3-0 for less than 10-point decision when loser does not score.

Bracket system: All major international competitions will use single elimination brackets with wrestlebacks if a wrestler has lost to a finalist.

Classification placement from seventh place and lower is established on the total number of positive classification points earned during the entire competition.

Weigh-ins: One weigh-in only per weight category. Competition will take place in that weight class in one day. However, no more than four matches is recommended in one day.

Superior decision: A 10-point difference terminates the match. However, if a pin is occurring, the pin will continue until the situation ends or a fall takes place. If the score is 7-0 (red) and red throws blue directly to his back for three points, then blue reverses red, the score is 10-1 and the match continues.

Danger position: Holding your opponent in a position of danger for five seconds (hand count) will earn one point.

Gut wrench: Only one gut wrench is allowed in any par terre position, unless any scoring occurs (1-2-3-5), then a gut wrench can be executed again. A gut wrench held in the danger position for five seconds for one point allows the wrestler to use the gut wrench again.

All passivity par terre positions will allow for one gut wrench. Any time the wrestler takes his opponent to the mat, a gut wrench can be scored.

INDEX

arm hook step-over 121
   shoulder drive 119
   sit-through 120
   step-over 122–123
   underhook 118
switch reversal 115

T

thigh block 103
three-quarter nelson 16–17
top man 3, 5
   tips 5
training
   graduated 136–139
   strength 136–139
training aids 139
turn-in 69, 70, 72, 73–74, 83
turn-in drill 81–82
turn-out 89, 90–91
turn-out drill 88

U

underhook 118
underhook arm lift 85–86

V

Van Horne, Bill xiii

W

weight loss diet 145–150
whizzer face-off 130–131

Bobby Douglas
is proud to be Co-Chairperson of the
ASICS® Wrestling Advisory Staff

Wrestling footwear was ASICS® first U.S. product introduced in 1959. Since then, ASICS® has become the shoe of choice among competitive wrestling athletes. For fall '93, ASICS® is complementing its performance-driven footwear line with the introduction of a wrestling apparel and accessories line, specifically designed for the wrestling enthusiast.

ASICS® Wrestling Advisory Staff

Bobby Douglas	1992 Olympic Coach, World Medalist, Captain 1988 Olympic Team
Dan Gable	NCAA, World, Olympic Champion
Bruce Baumgartner	NCAA, World, 2x Olympic Champion
Kenny Monday	NCAA, World, Olympic Champion
Dave Schultz	NCAA, World, Olympic Champion
Chris Campbell	NCAA, World Champion, Olympic Bronze Medalist
Bruce Burnett	US National Freestyle Coach
Tadaaka Hatta	NCAA Champion, USA Assistant Olympic Coach
Mike Houck	World Champion, USA National Greco-Roman Coach
Tricia Saunders	World and European Champion-Women
Kevin Jackson	NCAA All-American, World Champion, Olympic Champion
Zeke Jones	NCAA All-American, World Champion, Olympic Silver Medalist
Rodney Smith	Olympic Bronze Medalist, Greco-Roman

ASICS® Promotional Staff

Tiger Assoc.   50 Commercial Street
Bill Farrell   Plainview, New York 11803
Nick Gallo
Neil Duncan

Sponsorships

USA Wrestling, Official Equipment Sponsor
ASICS® Tiger / Oregon Classic
ASICS® Tiger Junior National Championships

☐ MC ☐ VISA Account # _____ Expiration Date _____

• Credit Card Orders call toll FREE 1-800-453-3960 or FAX to (515) 232-8820
• Checks/Money Orders - payable to: Sigler Printing & Publishing

Name _____

Address _____

City _____ State _____ Zip _____

Phone Number _____

Mail to: **Sigler Printing & Publishing**   Please send_____copies of ***Take It To The Mat*** @ $15.95 each $_____
        P.O. Box 887
        Ames, IA 50010-0887   Shipping ($1.50 per book) $_____
        Phone: (515) 232-6997   Iowa residents add 5% sales tax $_____
Please allow 2 - 3 weeks for delivery!   Local option tax add 1% $_____
Dealer discounts are available upon request.   Total $_____

☐ MC ☐ VISA Account # _____ Expiration Date _____

• Credit Card Orders call toll FREE 1-800-453-3960 or FAX to (515) 232-8820
• Checks/Money Orders - payable to: Sigler Printing & Publishing

Name _____

Address _____

City _____ State _____ Zip _____

Phone Number _____

Mail to: **Sigler Printing & Publishing**   Please send_____copies of ***Take It To The Mat*** @ $15.95 each $_____
        P.O. Box 887
        Ames, IA 50010-0887   Shipping ($1.50 per book) $_____
        Phone: (515) 232-6997   Iowa residents add 5% sales tax $_____
Please allow 2 - 3 weeks for delivery!   Local option tax add 1% $_____
Dealer discounts are available upon request.   Total $_____